WHEN TO
SPEAK UP
&
WHEN TO
SHUT UP

Dr. Michael D. Sedler

WHEN TO SPEAK UP

&

WHEN TO SHUT UP

Chosen
a division of Baker Publishing Group
Minneapolis, Minnesota

PRINCIPLES *for* CONVERSATIONS
YOU WON'T REGRET

Published by Chosen Books
11400 Hampshire Avenue South
Bloomington, Minnesota 55438
www.chosenbooks.com

Choosen Books is a division of
Baker Publishing Group, Grand Rapids, MI

Previously published under the title *When to Speak Up and When Not To*

ISBN 978-0-8007-9544-3

Printed in the United States of America

Library of Congress Cataoging-in-Publication Data is available for this title.

Cover design by Gearbox

This book is dedicated to those who were moved to speak up boldly in the midst of adversity and to those who were directed by God to remain silent while He moved in their presence.

I pray that this book will encourage each reader to be a voice in the wilderness of life: a voice of reason, of passion, of encouragement, of leadership, but most of all, of love and grace.

Contents

In Appreciation . . .

A special thank-you to Noreen, Debi and Alma. You encouraged me on days when I needed a pat on the back and a smile of friendship.

To the people at Chosen and Baker—Jane, Ann, Karen S., Karen V., Sheila and the rest. I am honored to be associated with such a professional group of people.

To my faithful wife, Joyce, thank you. You are an excellent wife and, truly, my crown.

one

Never Again

I was mute with silence, I held my peace even from good; and
my sorrow was stirred up.

Psalm 39:2

"I can't take it anymore. I am going to a lawyer to start divorce
proceedings." The words were sharp. Sandra was adamant in
her decision to divorce Ken, unwilling to listen to any contrary opinion. It appeared that a thirty-year marriage would
end in brokenness and hurt.

I was fresh out of graduate school with my master of social
work degree. While I was working full-time in the school system as a social worker, many people in our small community
approached me for counseling services. Directors of the local
mental health facility asked me to contract with them to help
with their unmanageable caseloads. In addition, several local
pastors called upon me to meet with some of their members
who needed counseling. It was through one of these church

contacts that I began counseling Sandra regarding her struggling marriage.

Sandra was an intelligent, energetic individual who worked in the local bank, and her husband, Ken, was a hard-working electrician. They had two children. Their older son was married and their daughter was a senior in high school. It seemed that the imminent "empty nest" was creating panic within Sandra. Most of Ken's leisure time was spent in front of the television or a newspaper, while Sandra was involved with housework and community activities. It had been years since the two of them had taken a vacation or enjoyed a weekend away. In Sandra's words, "Our marriage is dead. We are a married couple living separate lives." The thought of no children in the home and living with "just" Ken for the rest of her life was overwhelming.

I began meeting with Sandra on a weekly basis. She did not want to include her husband in our sessions, stating, "It wouldn't do any good." I attempted to guide her toward some sort of plan or focus that would bring freshness to the marriage. While her words were usually positive, her actions revealed a deeper truth; she was tired, hurt, discouraged and angry. Due to these emotions, Sandra was unwilling to allow for the possibility of change. She had Ken trapped in a prison of blame. I was prepared to challenge her in this area when she made her announcement.

It hit me like a bombshell. I knew that she was reluctant to press into a deeper understanding of her marriage, but she had never mentioned divorce. Being relatively new to the counseling arena, I searched my memory banks from my counseling classes to aid me in my response. Many textbooks discuss the potential damage from letting personal feelings impinge on one's counsel. The university professors concurred, emphasizing that as a counselor one should help the person find what he or she wants to do without imposing one's personal values.

And to a certain extent this is true. Individuals who come for counseling are often at a weak emotional state and susceptible to damage by those who would want to dominate them. But on the other hand, anyone who seeks help from a Christian counselor must expect that counselor to express any personal observations that support sound biblical teaching. In that regard, this situation—though in a professional setting—was not unlike any other situation in which we have to decide whether or not to speak our minds.

Still, on more than one occasion, the professors at the secular university chastised me for my personal Christian convictions. (I had refused to counsel a woman on how to obtain an abortion, for instance. Another time, I refused to support a man's involvement in pornography.)

So here I faced a dilemma. Should I follow the route set before me in the classroom and simply help her through the emotional impact of her decision? As I mentioned earlier, she was not willing to listen to any other options. Or should I state my personal conviction that divorce was not the plan of God for Sandra and Ken? I felt sure that God could heal their wounded marriage if they were willing to allow Him to guide their thoughts and actions.

After a quick analysis, my decision was made. I agreed to "help her" through the process of divorce. While uncomfortable with this decision, I felt resigned to the inevitable. She would meet with an attorney before our next session and share with me the results of that meeting.

As we started our session the following week, Sandra's body language showed weariness and resignation to a burdensome decision.

"The lawyer suggested I wait a year before I file for divorce," she said. "He felt that I should wait until my daughter graduates. If I proceed with the divorce now it will ruin her last year in school. So, I guess I will just hang on." With this, she began to sob. I had few words of consolation to offer. Honestly, I was relieved. I was glad that the lawyer had, at least temporarily, put the divorce on hold.

Later, my conscience gnawing at me, I shared the general facts of the case with my wife, Joyce. She posed a simple question: "Why didn't you give your perspective on the situation?" All my education, all my so-called wisdom was deflated. I realized that my voice had been non-existent. What had prevented me from speaking out? I cared about Sandra and Ken, yet I had accepted Sandra's insistence and agreed to help her with her decision. Perhaps professionally that was the correct course, but as a Christian counselor I was stunned that I had been willing to allow them to walk a road of pain and suffering without helping her see a different perspective. The weight of my silence stunned me.

The following days brought hours of prayer and soul-searching. I consider myself to be an individual who speaks his mind and is not afraid to share his thoughts. In fact, there are times my friends say I share too freely. (In other words, I need to keep my mouth closed.) I did not want to be a person who was overwhelmed or intimidated by situations and circumstances and unable to speak the truth of God.

A Life-Changing Experience

About two weeks later, a situation forever changed the way I view silence. The phone rang. It was Sandra. She was crying uncontrollably, her breath heaving with every word. As she spoke, my stomach knotted and a deep mourning filled my spirit. Ken had suffered a heart attack. He had collapsed in the living room while Sandra and her daughter were making breakfast. The paramedics pronounced him dead before he was even placed in the ambulance.

As my wife and I visited the mourning family, God quickened a disturbing thought to my mind. What if Sandra had filed for divorce? How would her children have coped not only with their father's death but also with the knowledge that she wanted to divorce him? And what of Sandra? Could she have lived with herself, thinking that the heart attack might have been related to the divorce? The ramifications could have been staggering. An incredible sense of relief and thankfulness came over me. I began to cry, thanking God for His mercy in this situation. It was difficult enough for the family to deal with the loss; having to factor into the equation the strain and stress of an impending divorce could have resulted in irreparable damage.

Yes, Sandra did have to come to terms with guilt over her feelings. She found solace in the fact, however, that she had never spoken of her intention to divorce Ken to anyone in the family, nor had she directed hostility toward Ken by using the idea of divorce as a weapon. God, in His sovereign way, spared Sandra—and me—years of "what-if" and "if only I had."

As I look back on that situation, I realize it was foundational for my beginning to understand the two sides of silence. The predicament I found myself in was not an uncommon problem: whether to share my personal feelings and risk being rebuffed or to remain silent, maintaining "peace" but not being true to myself. I remember that dilemma as if it were yesterday instead of twenty years ago. I now feel more prepared to ask God the question "Should I remain silent or should I speak?"

In the chapters of this book we will discuss the many sides of this question. We will explore ways that you can approach difficult situations with a godly intent and with a strategy that will enhance, not inhibit, communication. We will look at our motives for our decisions. We will address ways of dealing with peer pressure and authority—times you may feel uncomfortable about your position. We will investigate how an untimely word, a bad attitude or spiritual arrogance can create a wedge and a barrier to God's divine plan. We will learn how to make appeals and deal with anger and much more.

Because of a misuse of the spoken word, destinies have been derailed, disunity has replaced unity, nations have been destroyed. Our very lives, both physical and spiritual, depend upon our ability and willingness to speak out at the proper moment. And by the same token, silence can bring pain, destruction and the inevitable onslaught of sin. Or it can allow the time for God's healing power to work in a life.

It is my prayer that the following pages bring clarity and purpose into your life about when to speak up and when not to.

One Final Thought . . .

Mistakes and missed opportunities are a part of our growth cycle in life. There will be times when we speak out instead of remaining silent and there will be times we are silent when a voice should come forth. This book is not intended to create guilt or condemnation about those times we make errors in judgment. Instead, it is hoped that each one of us can evaluate our past choices and gain insights into our own personal lives, thus influencing our future decisions.

As I share my own personal triumphs, failures and shortcomings, I trust each reader will be encouraged to seek greater understanding into his or her own personal communication patterns. This truly is a book about love . . . loving one another enough to understand when we should remain silent and when we should speak—and if we do speak, doing so with words that promote and encourage further communication.

1. Think back over the years and find an example of one major lesson you have learned about not speaking up.
2. In examining your own personality and attitudes, do you have a tendency to be silent in troubling situations or to speak forth? Do you usually feel directed by God or by your own desires?

two

When Silence Isn't Golden

A time to keep silence, and a time to speak . . .

Ecclesiastes 3:7

The controversy of "keeping silent v. speaking out" is not a new one. It has, in fact, been examined for thousands of years. And its study is not isolated to one group, culture or religion.

While there are many authorities that speak on this topic, one of particular interest to me is the Talmud, a collection of literary works from many Jewish scholars written more than two thousand years ago. It spanned a period of seven hundred years, from approximately 200 B.C. to A.D. 500. Having been raised in a Jewish home, I heard often about the Talmud and the sage writings within the book. But it was not until the age of 22, when I turned my life over to Christ, that I first read the Talmud—and subsequently discovered its comments on the topic of silence. This subject is observed by A. Cohen in a book called *Everyman's Talmud* (Schocken Books, 1975):

> The misuse of the gift of speech is often the subject of warning. The Rabbis appreciated how unruly a member the tongue is, and for that reason, they declared, God provided it with exceptional controls. "The Holy One, blessed be He, said to the tongue, All the limbs of man are erect but you are horizontal; they are all outside the body but you are inside. More than that, I have surrounded you with two walls, one of bone and the other of flesh."
>
> Over much talking is deprecated. The proverb, "Speech is silver, silence golden," has its counterpart in the Talmud: "A word for a coin, silence for two"; "Silence is a healing for all ailments"; "Silence is good for the wise, how much more so for the foolish"; "All my days I have grown up amongst the wise, and I have found nought of better service than silence."

These Jewish scholars placed a high premium on silence. Likewise, many parents, teachers, historians and scholars seem to encourage silence, especially of younger individuals. The adage "It is better to be seen than heard" is a familiar one that discourages children from speaking out. Even historically the message seems to come through that silence is better than going against the grain and speaking up. To be an Abraham Lincoln, a John Wesley, a Martin Luther King, Jr., a Winston Churchill or an apostle Paul is to meet with resistance.

But is silence always golden?

What about the words in Scripture that plead with us to put words to our thoughts? Proverbs 8:1, for instance, shares how we need to cry out with wisdom and understanding: "Does not wisdom cry out, and understanding lift up her voice?" The psalmist beseeches God to hear his voice: "Give ear to my words, O Lord, consider my meditation. Give heed to the voice of my cry, my King and my God, for to You I will pray. My voice You shall hear in the morning" (Psalm 5:1–3). *Oh,*

God, our voices must not remain silent when You have directed us to speak!

The answer for us is not so perplexing: Both silence and speaking up have two sides. Both can be positive and appropriate. Both can also be negative and inappropriate. How do we distinguish?

In this chapter we will look at the issue of failing to speak when speaking is called for—those times when silence is *not* golden.

What are some of the reasons that a person might keep silent? He or she:

- May have nothing to add to a situation.
- May feel no one will listen.
- May feel intimidated by the environment and not feel comfortable expressing personal thoughts or convictions.
- May feel that it is none of his or her business to share personal impressions.
- May be fearful of repercussions.
- May simply not care.

Silence in the Garden

We need to examine the price of keeping silent when we should speak up—for there is often a cost. The best illustration comes from a story that is familiar to Christians and non-Christians alike. This story involves someone standing by, remaining silent, while another person made a destiny-changing decision. And not only did this decision alter the course of these two peoples' lives, it also had ramifications for their children and ultimately for the entire world for ages to come. This example of standing by and not speaking up is still relevant today, infiltrating schools, families, churches and businesses. Let us explore the story of Adam and Eve.

Now the serpent was more cunning than any beast of the field which the LORD God had made. And he said to the woman, "Has God indeed said, 'You shall not eat of every tree of the garden'?" And the woman said to the serpent, "We may eat the fruit of the trees of the garden; but of the fruit of the tree which is in the midst of the garden, God has said, 'You shall not eat it, nor shall you touch it, lest you die.'" And the serpent said to the woman, "You will not surely die. For God knows that in the day you eat of it your eyes will be opened, and you will be like God, knowing good and evil." So when the woman saw that the tree was good for food, that it was pleasant to the eyes, and a tree desirable to make one wise, she took of its fruit and ate. She also gave to her husband with her, and he ate.

Genesis 3:1–6

This story has been recounted over and over in homes, churches, synagogues, in books, magazines and on television. Always, it is the same. The snake deceived Eve and she ate. She then urged Adam to eat. He did so and the two were condemned to a life of hardship. But was it really that simple? Was Adam "tricked" into his actions? Or was silence involved, a time when a voice should have been heard but was not?

It is clear from Scripture that Adam was present when this exchange between Eve and the serpent took place. Note: "She also gave to her husband *with her,* and he ate" (verse 6, emphasis added). The New International Version of the Bible states it this way: "She also gave some to her husband, who was with her, and he ate it." You may find this hard to believe, but it is written plainly in each Bible. Go . . . take a look . . . I'll wait.

See, the Word of God is pointedly clear.

Adam heard the conversation, saw Eve's dilemma, but remained silent. All the while that his wife was being deceived, Adam watched and assessed the situation, but kept his thoughts to himself. He chose to be silent.

Can it really be that Adam, the first man, sat by passively while his wife was being tricked? Perhaps many teachings on the Garden scenario exclude this point because it seems more palatable that Eve alone was responsible. We would rather forget that her husband stood by as a silent observer. This is especially true for us men. We do not want to consider that a man's silence contributed to the most far-reaching deception in the history of the world. Heaven forbid!

Many Bible commentaries skim over verse six, choosing to ignore it rather than deal with it. Venerable Bible commentator Matthew Henry writes:

> It is probable that he was not with her when she was tempted, surely if he had, he would have intervened to prevent the sin.

Surely he would have! After all, why would anyone stand by, silent, while something negative happens to a person he loves? We would never do that. Would we? Yet, Adam did.

Wait a moment. Perhaps Adam did do something. "Then the man said, 'The woman whom You gave to be with me, she gave me of the tree, and I ate'" (Genesis 3:12). Adam did what people do best when feeling defensive: He blamed another person. Yes, Eve did take the forbidden fruit and eat it. And for this, historians, scholars, Sunday school teachers and ministers will forever speak of her sin. But what of Adam? Could he have prevented it? Does he have any culpability? It would seem that he carries some responsibility for watching his precious helpmate make a destructive decision without intervening.

And here we are today. How many of us have perpetuated the pattern established by Adam? Was the "original sin" Eve's eating the forbidden fruit or was it Adam's silence while his wife was deceived? Eve was his spouse, his companion, his friend, his co-laborer. Granted, the apostle Paul seems to indict Eve by stating that it was she, not Adam, who fell into deception and transgression (see 1 Timothy 2:13–14). But this seems to raise the question of Adam's culpability as well. True, Eve sinned greatly through her deception. True, Adam was *not* deceived. Does this not indicate, however, that he not only failed to protect her but ate with full knowledge of his actions? The book of Job speaks bluntly about Adam's behavior:

> "If I have covered my transgressions as Adam, by hiding my iniquity in my bosom, because I feared the great multitude, and dreaded the contempt of families, so that I kept silence and did not go out of the door . . . then let thistles grow instead of wheat, and weeds instead of barley."
>
> Job 31:33–34, 40

From a practical viewpoint, what could he have done? It was true that Eve had free will. There is no indication that she asked for Adam's opinion. Perhaps he would not have been able to dissuade her. But what do you think might have happened if Adam had said, "Eve, can we talk about this? You know what God has told us about this tree; do you really think this is a good idea? I don't feel comfortable with what you are about to do." His silence only allowed Eve to press forward without godly input. She still may have said, "Leave me alone," but at least he would have tried, and his counsel might have helped in his own decision. It is interesting that their eyes were opened only after *both* ate (see Genesis 3:7).

Adam was not being caring, protective or loving. On the contrary, he was being selfish, self-absorbed and perhaps fearful. Adam was silent. The price of his silence is staggering.

A Difficult Lesson

Janet is fourteen years old and is spending the next few months of her life in a drug rehabilitation program. Drugs and alcohol have absorbed the past year of her life. Naturally,

Janet never intended to become addicted to drugs. After all, she was "in control" and making her own choices. But soon, the drugs began to control her. How did this happen to a sweet, young, energetic junior high school girl?

Her parents, Sam and Carla, knew their daughter was starting to struggle in areas of her life. She was pushing the limits of basic household rules such as curfew, phone usage and chores. She started pulling away from her church youth group, a commitment she had always enjoyed. Her grades at school were slipping and, on numerous occasions, she had skipped classes. Janet's teachers and school counselor encouraged Sam and Carla to talk with professionals and to get involved in family counseling. Their pastor at church attempted to meet with them on several occasions. Prior to each meeting, however, they would call and cancel, stating that "things were getting better."

Privately, the parents expressed their fears regarding Janet's lifestyle decisions, but they refused to confront her and let her continue to "do her own thing." They felt Janet needed to make her own decisions and be responsible for her own behavior—and suffer the inevitable consequences. As each month passed, Sam and Carla saw their daughter spiral further into depression and isolate herself from friends and family. Before long Janet's parents became paralyzed by their inaction. The day came when the police arrested Janet (and several of her friends) for possession of drugs. After several weeks in the county detention facility, Janet was sentenced to ninety days in a residential drug rehabilitation program.

It was not that these parents had no concern for their daughter. Nor were they blind to her self-destruction. So, what kept their lips closed? Why were they unwilling to seek guidance from professionals? Basically, Sam and Carla did not want to interfere in their daughter's life. They felt Janet could make her own decisions; confrontation would only cause friction in the parent-child relationship. This conclusion is not uncommon in families and among friends. After all, "I don't want to interfere."

Excuses for Not Speaking Up

Shall we look a little closer to home? Do any of these phrases sound familiar?

- "It's his life. Let him make his own decisions."
- "She's old enough to make up her own mind."
- "I'm not his mother."
- "It's none of my business."
- "She knows the consequences of what she is doing."

For me, personally, these phrases are all too familiar. I have used them as excuses to be silent when friends and family would have benefited more by my speaking up.

Let's broaden this viewpoint just a bit. Please bear with me as my imagination takes a few liberties. Picture, if you will, Jesus looking out over the multitude. Here are people who need healing and release from demonic oppression, along with those who desperately want to know the Savior of the world. Now suppose that instead of His compassionate approach, Jesus says, "Yes, she does need a savior, but it really isn't My business to tell her what to do." Or "It's true, you are demon-possessed, but, hey, I'm not your mother." Or "I know he is lost to the world, but he is old enough to make his own decisions." Yes, these are ludicrous thoughts. However, we justify and rationalize our silence with just such phrases while loved ones fall into the clutches of Satan. Oh, the price of needless silence!

Is there ever a time when silence is appropriate? Absolutely, and we will discuss this in later chapters. However, if we remain quiet when someone needs to speak up, we may also need to accept some responsibility for the outcome. The Nuremberg war trials made a cogent, as well as legal, point on this issue. And biblically, if we use silence as self-protection, as a way to avoid confrontation or hard decisions, we do not glorify God. "The dead do not praise the LORD, nor any who go down into silence" (Psalm 115:17). Our silence will only create a spiritual death within us.

One Final Thought . . .

It can be quite difficult to balance godly discernment and fleshly impulse. In other words, there may be times that we feel the need to speak out, but we realize that our motives are not pure. And, realizing this, some of us choose to pull back and remain silent when guidance and correction are needed. Chapters that follow will take a closer look at our motives and habit patterns when talking to friends, family or authorities in our lives. The appendix describes my own battle with silence over a life-changing decision.

Do we want to continue the sin of Adam or break this cycle of sin? Why do we use silence as an excuse not to get involved? In the next chapter, we will address these areas as well as strategies for breaking out of the bondage of silence.

1. Like Adam, have you ever stood by and remained silent while knowing someone was making a bad decision? What was the impact of your silence?
2. What are some of the excuses you (or your friends) have used to remain silent?

three

A Kingly Voice

Keep quiet and people will think you a philosopher.

Latin proverb

Have you ever found yourself in a situation where a friend or loved one was choosing a direction in life that was contrary to what you thought was in his best interests? You saw things differently, yet you knew that if you spoke up you would risk being rebuffed or even verbally attacked. Did this possibility inhibit your voice? How should we approach these situations? One answer might be "Very carefully." As we look at this problem with spiritual eyes we find concise, clearly defined approaches.

The Bible includes many stories about just this type of scenario, times when a person sees an error in decisions being made and chooses to speak. One such account is found in the first book of Samuel, chapter 17. It is within this portion of Scripture that we find the story of David and Goliath. Let us examine how David, a man after God's own heart, responded to people who were making poor choices. Within this text of Scripture, we will see a process to follow when the "giant of silence" seeks to overwhelm us.

The Giant of Silence

We find David, a shepherd boy, tending the flock. His older brothers had joined with King Saul and the army of Israel in a battle against the Philistines. Twice a day, the champion of the Philistines, Goliath from Gath, taunted the Israelites with a verbal barrage:

> "Why have you come out to line up for battle? Am I not a Philistine, and you the servants of Saul? Choose a man for yourselves, and let him come down to me. If he is able to fight with me and kill me, then we will be your servants. But if I prevail against him and kill him, then you shall be our servants and serve us. . . . I defy the armies of Israel this day; give me a man, that we may fight together."
>
> 1 Samuel 17:8–10

The Bible states that King Saul and his army were dismayed and afraid.

One day, David's father, Jesse, told him to take some food to the Israelite army and check on his brothers. David obeyed and went to the frontline just as Goliath was coming forth to challenge the Israelites. What David saw shocked him. He was aghast at the fear he saw in the army of God. So David spoke up.

> Then David spoke to the men who stood by him, saying, "What shall be done for the man who kills this Philistine and takes away the reproach from Israel? For who is this uncircumcised Philistine, that he should defy the armies of the living God?"
>
> 1 Samuel 17:26

28

David challenged Goliath's authority, yet instead of support he heard only anger. And it came from his own family, one of his brothers.

> Now Eliab his oldest brother heard when he spoke to the men; and Eliab's anger was aroused against David, and he said, "Why did you come down here? And with whom have you left those few sheep in the wilderness? I know your pride and the insolence of your heart, for you have come down to see the battle."
>
> 1 Samuel 17:28

Word got around, however, and when King Saul heard of David's boldness, he sent for him. It appears that even Saul did not have the courage to challenge Goliath. Was it possible that a young shepherd boy could find the strength from God that the king of the Israelite army was lacking?

> Then David said to Saul, "Let no man's heart fail because of him; your servant will go and fight with this Philistine."
>
> 1 Samuel 17:32

David viewed the Israelites' situation from a different perspective. He was probably the youngest man there and he was not even a part of the army. His older brothers felt, no doubt, that it was inappropriate for him to speak out and challenge the men of Israel. Yet David was seeing through spiritual eyes.

This was not an impulsive moment on his part, a chance to antagonize his brothers. He had done that in the past, perhaps, out of anger, frustration or simply immaturity. Certainly, there had been sibling quarrels, bickering, wrestling and teasing amongst the family of Jesse. But this was different. David had been prepared for this day. He had been trained "for such a time as this" and he knew it.

I would like to mention here that while David was strong about speaking up during this time of his life, this was not

29

always the case. Do you remember the story of David's refusal to confront his son Amnon over the raping of Tamar (see 2 Samuel 13)? And what about his unwillingness to embrace Absalom for many years (see 2 Samuel 14)? David again chose silence over having a voice when Shimei challenged him (see 2 Samuel 16).

Our lives are full of complexities, complete with contradictions and confusion over choices we must make each day. Just as David made both good and bad decisions, we, too, can fall prey to indecision and double-minded thinking. Why was the situation with Goliath different for David? What had he done to ensure that he would respond in a godly fashion? What prevented him from falling into the typical trap of sibling rivalry and losing his focus?

Let's look at how David prepared for that day and his godly method of confronting the Israelites.

1. David's personal experiences prepared him to be in the midst of battle.

While not a member of the Israelite army, David was nonetheless battle-tested and ready.

> But David said to Saul, "Your servant used to keep his father's sheep, and when a lion or a bear came and took a lamb out of the flock, I went out after it and struck it, and delivered the lamb from its mouth; and when it arose against me, I caught it by its beard, and struck and killed it. Your servant has killed both lion and bear."
>
> 1 Samuel 17:34–36

David knew what it was like to be attacked, to feel fear. He also knew what it meant to protect something precious.

As a parent I know the feeling of wanting to protect my children. If something or someone threatens them, I rise up to prevent them from injury or harm. The army of Israel had been given the honor of protecting the people, yet they were shrinking back. David saw this and it violated the sense of shepherding so ingrained in his spirit. When David spoke out, it was not from ignorance or a lack of understanding. He understood the battle.

Do we have personal experience in the battles we undertake? If not, are we willing to receive guidance and counsel?

During my teenage years I spent the summers working at a warehouse in Phoenix, Arizona. I was responsible for loading and unloading trucks carrying lumber, hardware and electrical supplies. The days were filled with hard, rigorous work as trucks would arrive one after the other.

Our boss, Mac, was a short, heavyset man who had spent the majority of his life working in that warehouse. He had a no-nonsense attitude and did not enjoy some of the pranks that the younger workers, such as myself, brought into "his domain." Many of us felt the sting of his negative comments regarding our work ethic, long hair or musical preference. This is not too different from issues of today. I guess some things never change.

By the summer following my high school graduation, I was a seasoned veteran of the warehouse. After all, I had worked there for a grand total of six months (two summer stints). One particularly hot and grueling day, as the trucks continued to come in and out of the warehouse yard, several of us decided we had a better way of unloading the trucks.

You see, we were taught one specific method for unloading trucks and we were expected to follow it. Mac had driven that point home several times. He demanded we unload a portion of a truck, and then move the truck to the next unloading dock. The workers at that dock would unload their portion and move the truck along to another unloading dock. This suddenly seemed to us tedious and, after all, we were more creative, younger and smarter (remember, I was now a high school graduate). Certainly those of us who were college-bound knew more than a man who had spent all his years in a warehouse. We decided to unload each truck completely and not use this step-by-step method. Each unloading dock would completely empty one truck instead of only a portion.

The first truck or two went well. But, after a couple of hours of using our new method, we began to see a backlog of trucks. They seemed to be coming out of nowhere. Instead of having one truck waiting to be unloaded at each dock, we had two or three. Suddenly, we heard the booming voice of Mac echoing throughout the warehouse. "What's going on here?" This was going to be an ugly scene.

Mac helped us for the next few hours as we reverted back to his system. The trucks were soon on their way and Mac sat down with our team. But instead of expressing anger toward us, he helped us learn a valuable lesson. Mac explained carefully and thoughtfully that he, too, had thought there was a better way. In fact, some years ago he had tried it the same way we did that day, with the same results. He shared that while we brought zeal and energy to the job, he had the experience, the testing over the years and knew what worked and what did not. From that day forward, we followed his methods and had few problems on the job.

Too often we speak emotionally or act impulsively, not having assessed the whole situation. While we may disagree with what we see, we must be sure that our actions are valid. The fact that we do not like what is occurring around us does not give us permission to come against it. Simply because David did not like what Goliath was saying was no reason for David to challenge his older brothers. He needed to understand the "big picture" of the battle, and he did.

My children have not always agreed with the rules my wife and I have set for them, but their limited experiences do not give them sufficient background to understand what is appropriate in many areas (bedtime, curfews, where they go, whom they go with, etc). As they have grown, their understanding has increased. Their more mature requests for increased freedom have been met with appropriate responses from us. Maturity and experience have made the difference. Not long ago one of my sons said jokingly, "Dad, don't you think my bedtime should be extended? After all, I am 29 years old." Naturally, I listened to him!

David knew the cost of losing a battle. The "sheep" would have been injured, even destroyed. Due to his understanding and experience, David was able to respond to the challenges from Goliath with authority.

2. David desired to be a servant.

David wanted to encourage his brothers and the other soldiers. His heart held no contempt, jealousy or criticism. He had reverence and honor for the Israelite army and its king. It was not his desire to mock them or to humiliate them. David was at the frontline because he was doing his duty—serving!

> Then Jesse said to his son David, "Take now for your brothers an ephah of this dried grain and these ten loaves, and run to your brothers at the camp. And carry these ten cheeses to the captain of their thousand, and see how your brothers fare, and bring back news of them." . . . So David rose early in the morning, left the sheep with a keeper, and took the things and went as Jesse had commanded him.
>
> 1 Samuel 17:17–18, 20

David's sole motivation in his obedience was to bless and serve his father and brothers.

Too often we feel that we must elevate ourselves to a person's level of authority or position in order to speak truth into his or her life. The story of David teaches us that this is not necessary. In fact, when we are willing to pour into the lives of others through obedience, God often opens their ears. Remember the story of Naaman the leper (see 2 Kings 5). He refused to wash in the Jordan River when directed by Elisha's messenger. However, when Naaman's servants, the soldiers under his command, spoke to him about being obedient he listened. Why? They were his subordinates, his servants, not his equal. But Naaman saw their faithfulness to serve and to care for his needs. He knew they would only speak words intended to help him.

If you want to maximize the possibility of others "hearing" your voice, it is imperative they see your heart of service. Too often, the heart people see in others is the heart of "self-service," which breeds suspicion and animosity. This had apparently grown in David's brother. Even though David was in a place of servitude, Eliab was filled with mistrust. He accused David of appearing on the battlefield because of his "pride and insolence." Fortunately, David's motives were pure, giving him confidence to speak out and allowing King Saul to see beyond the negative comments of Eliab and into the strength of David. Again, if you feel compelled to confront a situation, it is imperative to step forth with a heart of humility and service.

3. David asked questions to get the "big picture."

He asked about Goliath, wanting to know who he was and what right he had to come against Israel. He also wanted to know what rewards were being offered to the man who killed Goliath. While Eliab made his angry accusations against David for asking such questions, David shrugged it off. It is likely that Eliab felt defensive, perhaps even convicted over his own fear (see 1 Samuel 17:24). David continued probing. "It was only a question," he said. "Isn't there a reason (or cause) to ask these things?" David then turned to others and asked again, "What shall be done for the man who kills this Philistine and takes away the reproach from Israel?"

Here we see David's desire to get a sense of how others perceived the situation. This gave him insight into the emotional status of the soldiers. Were they afraid? Were they waiting for someone to take charge? Did they think Saul should do something? By asking these questions, David was able to understand the situation better. He was then able to formulate his own ideas and decide how to proceed.

Notice also that he did not focus on the negative—why his brothers were scared or why the people did not do something. Instead, he focused on the positive and on the immediate situation.

When we feel the desire to speak up in a particular situation, it is important to understand each nuance as completely as possible. Too often, we blunder ahead and find out that we did not have all the facts. Asking questions is an excellent way to garner information before formulating a plan. It also shows those who are involved that we are interested in their ideas and thoughts.

Case in point: A few weeks ago, several of us were discussing a new movie. Greg walked into the room and, upon hearing the name of the movie, launched into a quick explanation of the plot and a critique of the ending. Unfortunately, a minute or so before Greg came into the room, we had all discovered that we had not seen the movie but knew that it had a surprise ending. We had just decided to go later that day to see it. Once Greg finished, we all looked at one another with a "Well, there goes that movie" shrug. When Greg found out that we had not seen it, he felt bad about ruining the ending. We often speak words without understanding the situation.

When confronted with the dilemma of whether to speak or be silent, be sure you have ample information with which to make a wise decision. Ask questions. Listen to the responses. Evaluate the atmosphere of the discussion and whether or not that particular moment is the proper time to share what is on your heart. You may decide to wait for a better time, even though what you are sensing is important.

We have been doing some remodeling around our house. We live on a two-acre piece of property and are planning to purchase a couple of horses. In order to prepare for this, we are spending many hours building fences. While we are excited about how nice the fences look, the project has been tedious and time-consuming. We usually get up early in the morning, go at it for an hour or two before work, then return to fence-building in the evening.

I am the type of person who likes to complete a project once I get started. Don't interrupt me for dinner, for phone calls, for anything; just let me go for it. When Joyce and I were first married, she did not understand this about me. It created times of friction between us. For instance, if I planned to work for three hours, but Joyce had planned to work only for one hour, we had problems. In a fit of frustration I would ask her why she was stopping. In her mind, it was time to stop. All my "speaking up" did not help. She felt guilty if she rested or moved on to another project because I kept going.

Through discussions, miscommunications and more discussions, we realized that we were making assumptions and not gaining enough information about the other's perspective. We gradually realized that we needed to ask more questions and get more information about the other's perspective if we were going to work harmoniously.

Now, we usually set a time frame before we get started. Joyce will let me know if we are going to have to quit in an hour because of a prior commitment. She will remind me that at a specific time she has planned a special dinner. (Of course, all her dinners are special!) I may mention an appointment we have in two hours. We have learned effective ways to help prepare the atmosphere ahead of time.

Through this personal experience I have also seen how timing is critical. After Joyce has spent a day of shopping, carpooling kids to games, doing laundry and an assortment of other tasks, it is not wise for me to comment about a particular shirt not being ironed. Timing, timing, timing. Test the temperature of the water before jumping in. In other words, ask questions to get the information you need so that you can better pick and choose the appropriate times to bring up issues.

4. David fought the problem (Goliath), not the people.

Upon hearing of the challenge from Goliath, David responded, "Who is this uncircumcised Philistine, that he should defy the armies of the living God?" (1 Samuel 17:26). David did not question his brothers or the other men as to their lack of courage, even in the face of their obvious fear. David chose to attack Goliath with his words. Even when he came face to face with Goliath, he did not set himself up as better or more worthy than the other soldiers.

> Then David said to the Philistine, "You come to me with a sword, with a spear, and with a javelin. But I come to you in the name of the LORD of hosts, the God of the armies of Israel, whom you have defied. . . . All this assembly shall know that the LORD does not save with sword and spear; for the battle is the LORD's, and He will give you into *our hands.*"
>
> 1 Samuel 17:45, 47, emphasis added

Notice how David spoke in a corporate manner, including his fellow soldiers in the impending victory.

Too often, when we disagree we tend to attack people and put them on the defensive. David's desire was to challenge their thinking by helping the Israelites see the awesome power of God. When we find ourselves in a place of confrontation, it behooves us not to come against an individual, but to help people expand their perspectives and see the possibilities in God.

It is also worth noting that David offered to fight the giant as a last resort. He watched as all the other soldiers refused to respond to the taunts. His desire was not to be noticed, to be the hero. He simply felt that Goliath was getting away with something contrary to the purposes of God. David was unwilling to remain silent when a voice was needed to rise up against the enemy.

Applying the Principles of David

Daniel and Joey were close friends, yet they often found themselves in heated arguments. They seemed to disagree about everything—the best baseball player, the fastest car, the hottest music group. Both Daniel and Joey tried to prove their points with degrading comments about the knowledge and experience of the other one: "You don't know anything about baseball" or "You listen to that kind of music?" Like many of us they both could have learned a lot from examining the life of young David and his approach to conflict. David learned early to point out a deficiency and encourage a solution. Even in his teenage years David tried to lead by encouragement and example—godly qualities found in leaders or, in David's case, found in a king.

Let's look briefly at these principles once more.

First, when we feel a need to speak up, it is helpful to examine our own lives. What type of knowledge base do we have in this area? Are we sharing from a foundation of experience? While it is not always necessary to have a great deal of experience or knowledge in order to have a strong belief system, it may affect the receptivity of the persons with whom we are sharing. The more comfortable we are with personal experiences that support a belief system, the less defensive and aggressive we will be in our speech.

Second, in times of confrontation or disagreement, we are most effective when we are motivated to encourage and educate. That is, my motive for sharing is not to convince others, but to give an additional perspective and broaden their understanding. I feel I am providing a service by helping them gain information and additional viewpoints, thus allowing them to make a more informed decision. When we are caught up with "proving" something, it often turns into a power struggle.

Third, as David did, we need to ask questions, being careful that we have all the information and pertinent facts. As the years go by, I become better at asking questions. Sometimes in meetings I will ask several questions prior to giving my opinion. The more information I obtain and the greater the breadth of my perspective, the more accurate my responses will be. Too often, we feel as though we need to give a quick answer to show how much we know. I am convinced that a person who asks educated, informed questions is the one who will appear most knowledgeable. Let me clarify this point with a couple of examples:

Rather than saying this: "You need to remember that the Bible tells us not to be offended and let the sun go down on our anger," try this: "I see that you are too angry to discuss the issue with your husband. It would seem a time of prayer and thinking is in order. Do you see yourself discussing this with him in the next few days?" Asking this question is much more effective than preaching at the person.

And rather than stating this: "Pornography is a sin and it will only separate you further from God," try this: "It appears that pornography has become a stronghold in your life. Is this an area you desire to break free from? If so, I would be willing to walk alongside you as you seek counsel." Again, this lets the person know that you see the area of struggle and are willing to be a part of the solution. In both of these cases the initial statement is certainly true, but it may yield only defensiveness and anger in the person you wish to reach.

And fourth, David showed us the key to taking a contrary position without causing a fight. He did not attack the people; instead he stood with them in battle. In my work in the school system I found that parents and teachers were often in conflict over the students. Yet all of the adults involved had a similar goal—to help the children. If a problem is addressed with accusation and innuendo, the only results are frustration and defensiveness. *Instead of attacking one another, we need to attack the problem.*

Before confronting a family member or a friend, it may be best to ask yourself a few questions:

- Have I prayed about the situation and for those involved?
- Am I the right person to speak into this situation?
- Am I attacking the person or helping him see a problem?
- Do I have any solutions for the situation?
- Do I need to own some of the problem? What part?
- Am I attempting to exalt myself? Am I speaking in a condescending manner?
- What is my motive for confronting this situation?
- Am I willing to change, to be challenged or to support an alternative decision?
- Am I able to find peace if the situation does not change?

Notice how David did not respond in a defensive manner when challenged. His demeanor and approach opened up the way for King Saul to allow him to fight Goliath. I wonder how different the outcome might have been if instead King Saul had seen David bickering with his brothers, shouting, calling one another names.

One Final Thought . . .

Now is a good time to evaluate our own motivations for speaking up. We must examine our own hearts and personal ambitions. No, we do not want to remain silent as Adam did, nor do we want to withdraw as the Israelites did. Should we then "boldly go where no man has gone before" without thinking or planning? Is there a balance between silence and speaking? As we continue in our study may we seek direction and courage to make a change in the world around us.

1. Are there times you have followed the pattern of young David?
2. What is the most difficult part about confronting family or loved ones? Do you have a strategy or approach to help overcome this barrier?

four

Communication Breakdown

Nicodemus said to Him, "How can a man be born when he is old? Can he enter a second time into his mother's womb and be born?"

"Fired? What for?" Scott was practically shouting. "Just because I don't agree with you?"

Barbara, the owner of the small business where Scott worked, was clearly shaken. Scott, an employee for several years, had reached the position of manager at one of her stores. Now, she was firing him. It all seemed like a blur to her. How had this happened? What went wrong in her relationship with Scott that caused him to do such damage to her reputation and her small company?

To Barbara, the problem had just surfaced. It was new and fresh. But to Scott it had been simmering for many months. Actually, it had started well over a year before when Scott asked for a few days off. His parents were coming for a visit and he wanted to spend some extra time with them. When he approached Barbara, she reminded him that they would soon be taking inventory and how busy it was during that time of year. Though Scott felt there were solutions to this situation, he simply agreed to work his regular shifts.

Imagine his surprise when he learned that another worker was given a day off to go to a football game. And even Barbara was not in the store each of those days. He had been a faithful worker. What more did she expect from him?

Unfortunately, Scott did not go and talk to Barbara about his feelings. Instead, he let his anger fester. He began to question her decisions and management style and was often heard mumbling about his job. He was bitter and hurt, yet refused to approach Barbara and point out the inequities he saw. And when he did try to talk with her on various occasions about specific customer orders, he always felt as though she was not really present. The phone rang constantly, she worked on scheduling while she talked and she checked her watch periodically.

When new displays arrived one holiday season, Scott considered it a waste of money. He made a few comments about money being spent on decorations that could have been used for salary raises. When Barbara decided to keep the store open later during summer weekends, Scott saw this as taking advantage of the workers. After all, it was summer and he wanted to go to the lake.

Even with all these thoughts in his head, Scott was still a diligent worker. And when Barbara approached him about being a manager he was pleased. *Finally!* he thought. *Now I can implement my own plans and turn this store into something special.* Though Scott was a bit overwhelmed the first month or two, he did not ask for guidance or help from Barbara. He wanted to do it on his own without her interference. It was in his second month of managing that another incident drove the wedge between them deeper.

Scott ordered new inventory for an upcoming sale. He did not tell Barbara. As it turned out, he could have used extra inventory at one of the other stores; now, there was an overabundance of stock. When Barbara found out about this error, she promptly called Scott into her office. It had been a particularly difficult month financially and Barbara was frustrated with the additional stock on hand. In her anger, she lashed out at Scott, stating that he was not a team player and had better "shape up" if he was going to make it in business.

Now every little difference between Barbara and Scott became magnified in his mind. He questioned many of the owner's decisions openly—with other employees and even with customers. Barbara began to realize the extent of the trouble between them when a couple of new employees were having their thirty-day evaluations. They repeated several of the comments Scott was making and expressed how the atmosphere at the store he managed was incredibly uncomfortable. Barbara was even more surprised when one of her best customers called her and questioned the integrity of the business and the "price-gouging" taking place. In fact, he threatened to take his business elsewhere if Barbara did not reevaluate her pricing procedures.

When she hung up the phone, she was shocked. She had just learned that Scott was complaining of "price-gouging" to other employees. Was he making this comment to the customers as well? Over the next couple of days, Barbara received two more complaints from customers.

Enough was enough! Barbara knew she had to take action. Her business and reputation were being destroyed from within. This could go on no longer. As difficult as it might be, she would have to confront Scott and fire him.

Taking Stock

The above story is all too common. Individuals find themselves in the position of being verbally attacked by someone, often in a covert manner. A disgruntled employee, fellow worker, carpooler—whoever—finds something to complain about. There might be legitimacy in the complaints and a need to evaluate certain areas, but when the communication takes a destructive approach, little positive change will occur.

The week following Scott's dismissal was difficult for Barbara. She wrestled with her decision but was more taken aback by the lack of communication between Scott and her. It was during this week of introspection that Barbara called me. She asked to meet with me and go over the situation. She wanted some feedback.

After we had talked for several hours, Barbara realized that her demeanor and attitude had discouraged Scott from talking with her about the problems he faced. She had unwittingly presented herself as a lone authority, one who wanted little feedback from employees. This was also the type of person she hired—one who did not want feedback or guidance from his employer. Scott and Barbara were similar—bright, competent, creative but unwilling to share ideas and work together for a common goal.

This story had a happy conclusion. Barbara met with Scott and discussed her new understanding of the situation. She apologized and asked for Scott's forgiveness for not being more open to his ideas. Likewise, Scott took ownership of his negative comments and not coming directly to Barbara. He realized his words had caused an atmosphere of criticism and divisiveness among the employees. Barbara offered to hire Scott back. He anxiously accepted with one proviso. He asked for the opportunity to speak to each employee and admit his error in judgment. Since then I have had a couple of meetings with both Barbara and Scott to establish new procedures and structures that enhance communication within the business.

Does this type of scenario sound familiar to you? Have you ever found yourself on one side or the other of a communication breakdown? What can we learn from this about the failure to speak up? Let's see how we can prevent this type of breach within a work, family or church setting. In the next chapter we will deal specifically with approaching authority figures.

Conversation Guidelines

Take a moment and look at your own life. Examine situations where you have chosen not to approach someone with whom you disagree. Did this have any impact on your attitude or perspective about the person? The job? The family? Here are several options for times when we need to speak up about a troubling situation. These few principles can help keep problems from escalating into communication breakdowns.

1. Establish procedures for communication before a problem rises.

If you are in a supervisory position, develop a procedure for people to reach you. Would you prefer phone calls, e-mails or personal meetings? When someone has a question, should he contact you directly or present the questions during weekly meetings? If you are in a subordinate position, do you know the procedure that you should follow in such a case?

Do you take the time to listen to opposing ideas and suggestions? Or do you have tunnel vision? Are you in such a hurry to complete tasks that you refuse to examine other ideas and approaches? Are you approachable? That would be a great question to ask your fellow workers. And if you are a supervisor or business owner, it should be a mandatory question for each member of your staff and employees.

This principle applies not only to business, of course, but to every aspect of life.

Take marriage. Busy spouses forget to be accessible. One spouse, usually the wife (sorry, guys, but it is the truth), becomes discouraged, feeling isolated and alone. She does not sense that her husband wants to communicate on the same level she does. She asks a question and wants a dialogue on the scale of *War and Peace*. Instead, she gets the *Reader's Digest* condensed version of *Lassie, Come Home*.

Soon, walls are built between husband and wife.

My wife and I know several married couples who take time every week to go have a cup of coffee together, just to talk and share about their lives. We have a number of friends who go out once a week on a "date night." If you are married, consider sitting down with your spouse and establishing a procedure for regular communication. If you think it will just happen on its own, well, my countless hours of marriage counseling and personal experiences tell me otherwise.

The same is true for parents. Do your kids know they can approach you with contrary ideas? Now, wait a minute, I know we all think we are open to our children's ideas, but what do *they* think? Take some time and ask your children if they feel they can talk to you about issues in life. How about topics such as drugs, sex, money, relationships? May they ask questions, even disagree with you?

Honesty speaks volumes. If parents tell their kids to be honest and tell the truth but Dad or Mom lies to the boss—"I can't come to work today because I'm sick"—or to their friends—"I can't help you move tomorrow because I have other plans"—the result is confusion within a child's life. How would you, as a parent, respond to your children if they questioned certain aspects of your life?

Naturally, we see the same problems within the Church. Leaders become isolated and insulated. People get frustrated with the leadership, yet cannot find a pathway to express their concerns. This is especially true in larger churches. Leaders in smaller churches (a hundred people or so) appear to be more accessible. Then as that church or organization grows, more layers develop between those on a decision-making level and those who are affected by those decisions.

The church where I serve as an assistant pastor started with a small group of people. For many years this original core group met regularly. They became close-knit and used informal communication patterns. As the years progressed, the group expanded into a church of seven hundred members. At one time anyone with a concern could sit down over a cup of coffee with a senior leader and discuss a problem; it is now more difficult. As groups increase more demands are placed on each person. Now seven hundred people, not fifty, pull on the senior pastor. And even though other individuals round out the leadership structure, those who grew up with direct access to the senior leader still desire it. This is not bad, it is just not always practical.

I imagine there are those who were used to quick and easy communication with the current President of the United States. After all, prior to the Oval Office it was much easier for friends or family to call or make an appointment. Now international affairs, state emergencies and federal budgetary issues are daily burdens. While the President might desire a nice impromptu get-together with friends, barriers restrict this type of communication.

An interesting example of a preset communication procedure is found in the Bible in the book of Esther. There was a plot afoot to kill all the Jews and a man named Mordecai discovered it. When this information was shared with Queen Esther, herself of Jewish descent, she did not feel free to go before the king and plead her case. A set procedure had to be followed in order to approach him.

> "All the king's servants and the people of the king's provinces know that any man or woman who goes into the inner court to the king, who has not been called, he has but one law; put all to death, except the one to whom the king holds out the golden scepter, that he may live."
>
> Esther 4:11

I am not suggesting any husbands try this particular procedure at home or that supervisors try it at work! I have, however, worked in a few places where it felt as though this procedure were in place! The idea of going and talking to the supervisor, without his specific summons, was unthinkable. I had the impression that "his time is too important to be taken up by someone like me."

Do you have some kind of guidelines in place with family and friends so that communication can flow? Do your children know how and when to communicate with you? Have you stopped being so busy that your spouse needs to make an appointment with you? Do your coworkers appreciate your commitment to building relationship?

If you fail in these areas, the stifled emotions will ultimately blow up. The key is being certain that those people who are a significant part of your life understand the communication process.

2. Do not shut down and hold feelings or ideas inside.

If you face untenable or confusing situations you must speak out. It is possible to disagree with people and still be positive, respectful and supportive. The way in which you approach others is critical to the success of the conversation. I propose the following strategies:

- Plan to go directly to the person with whom you disagree. Whether or not he agrees with you does not diminish the importance of sharing your feelings. Remember, if you hide or stuff your feelings, they do not improve. Eventually, bitterness and frustration will result.
- Ask to meet personally with the individual. Set up an appointment. Avoid a quick exchange at the snack bar or after a service at church. Let the person know you

would like a few minutes of her time to discuss something important.

- When you share your concerns, be sure to emphasize that you are giving *your* impressions and *your* ideas. Do not implicate others or suggest that "everyone" sees it your way. That will put the individual, particularly a boss or supervisor, on the defensive.
- Share positive comments first. We all like to hear positives and they will help to balance any negative comments.
- Be open to feedback. The person may know more about the situation than you do.
- Be prepared to give possible suggestions or solutions when discussing problems. My senior pastor says that he appreciates it when I come to him with ideas to solve problems or ways to work together toward a solution. He is then able to weigh my suggestions with other plans he may already have.
- Do not attack the person or insinuate that you would do a better job. This is not a competition and should be kept out of the realm of "who is better."

My son is presently playing baseball at his college. He was not given many opportunities to play during a recent two-game series. He was frustrated over his lack of playing time. After we talked, he chose to follow the above procedures. Not only did he have an excellent meeting with his coach, he came away with a new appreciation for keeping communication open.

As for Barbara and Scott, both felt that weekly employee meetings would be beneficial. These meetings included all store employees and gave the owner and managers a chance to discuss new ideas and policies with the workers. They also provided a forum for questions or concerns. The meetings allowed management to examine the direction of the business and gain valuable input from the employees.

Barbara asked me to speak to her employees about gossip and the destructive results of not working through areas of offense. I gave each employee a copy of my book *Stop the Runaway Conversation*, which addresses issues of gossip and negativity. In retrospect, this was a successful learning time for all those involved, especially for Barbara and Scott.

3. During a meeting or conversation, be available emotionally and mentally.

I have been in meetings and gatherings in which people were available only physically and clearly were not giving their undivided attention. Subtle (and not so subtle) cues like checking your calendar or keeping one eye on the television are not going to encourage people to communicate with you.

What a lesson we can learn from Jesus' meetings with people! When He entered the Temple and people came to Him, Jesus sat down and was readily available to teach them. When He was on His way to heal the daughter of Jairus, He took the time to talk to a woman who needed healing. He gave her His full attention because she had the faith to touch the hem of His garment. Jesus did not let "other plans" get in the way of being available to those who needed Him.

Do we take this kind of time for others? Even when we are busy with pressing thoughts or activities? What do your meetings with others look like? On second thought, what would you like them to look like? Listed below are some simple guidelines to enhance your communication.

- Avoid interruptions. Take the phone off the hook, have another person answer it or find a place where you will not be bothered. If you have a cell phone or pager, put it on "silent" mode. Allow it to take messages.

- If necessary state a time frame. "We have about thirty minutes. Let's get started." Or "I have to leave the house in about twenty minutes. Does that give us enough time?" This allows the person to know how much to share and how quickly. If the time frame is not sufficient, it might be necessary to reschedule.

- In a business setting, take notes. This will not only help you remember what was said but let the other people know that their comments are important.

- Listen. Listen. Listen. There will be plenty of time to share your perspective and feelings. If the other person (whether a child, spouse, friend or colleague) initiated the meeting, let him or her talk freely.

- Be open to new ideas. The person may share difficult issues. The areas may be personal. You may disagree. It is okay to allow the other person the opportunity to express concerns, even if the perception seems not to be accurate. Once the person has finished, ask if he would like a response. Almost always he will; that is usually why he came to you. This gives you ample opportunity to state your opinions.

4. Set up a follow-up meeting, if necessary.

Too often, once a meeting is over we wash our hands of the problem. This can lead to a sense of incompleteness and lack of closure. It is almost like walking out of the movies during the last five minutes of a murder mystery. Most mysteries include a final scene in which the detective ties up the loose ends. A follow-up meeting does this as it offers clarity and closure to previous discussions. Individuals can share their reflections on past discussions and ask clarifying questions.

I recently met with my son Aaron regarding an area of his life. He was feeling singled out by teachers over an issue that had taken place at his school. We had an excellent discussion and I encouraged him to evaluate his thinking. Granted, the attention was making him feel uncomfortable, but was there truth to what he was being told by his authorities? Sometimes, the delivery of the message can interfere with the message itself. After we finished, I asked if we could talk about it again in a couple of days to see how he had processed everything. He readily agreed. During our next meeting, he shared some wonderful insights he had received as he had internalized our talk. I was impressed and pleased by the maturity he showed. I might never have known his insights if a follow-up meeting had not occurred.

Most people are anxious to connect again, especially if they feel the second meeting will produce greater understanding and communication. Avoid giving the impression that the purpose of another meeting is to chastise or correct their behavior or attitude. This will discourage any desire for a follow-up meeting. Just because someone agrees to meet does not mean he is open to communication. Be sure to let the person know that your desire for follow-up is to continue the process of communication. It is not to "check up" on him but offer further resources.

One Final Thought . . .

Our goal should be to encourage communication and help people to find a way to speak their thoughts. Unfortunately, we spend more time "doing" than "listening." We were given two ears for a reason. (No. Not to hold up our hats!) Communication breakdowns discourage people from sharing their thoughts and ideas, and create opportunities for offense, bitterness and misunderstanding. Hurtful silence within a family, a church, a business or among friends can be devastating. Commit yourself to finding new ways to encourage discussions and communication among your personal and business contacts.

1. When involved in a difficult conversation, do you fall into communication traps? Name a few.
2. Did the list of conversation guidelines bring up any areas of growth for your conversations?

five

A Question
of Authority

In the end, we will remember not the words of our enemies,
but the silence of our friends.

Martin Luther King, Jr.

We are going to explore a difficult topic, one that creates
confusion in families, in businesses and the local church. It
involves relating to another person who is an authority in your
life. It is one thing to challenge a friend, coworker or peer,
but when confrontation involves a boss, parent, teacher or
religious leader, we often have second thoughts about speaking up. After all, this person has the ability to fire us, to take
away privileges or even to stifle personal growth. Who wants
to upset that person!

So instead of dealing in a godly manner with our misgiv-
ings, we fall into the trap of misguided silence, which often
leads to gossip or murmuring. This presents its own unique

and difficult problems. In order to avoid the many pitfalls of failing to speak up when we should, let's examine the difference between "questioning"—a negative approach to those in authority—and "asking questions"—the right response to our concerns.

First, what is *questioning?* What does it look like? Have I ever been involved in this type of interaction?

Questioning

Note first of all that not all questions are necessarily a form of "questioning." Many times, we are honestly trying to gain further understanding. This will be discussed later in the chapter as we talk about "asking questions." However, when the motive is to create disunity, to override another's opinion with our own or to prove our points, our motives are wrong and fall into the category of "questioning authority." Questioning is a confrontational form of conversation that is filled with suspicion, lack of trust and accusations and puts people on the defensive.

Spiritually, those of us with a questioning attitude create a barrier to God. We do the same thing with Him. We ask question after question, not hearing His response or accepting the answers we do hear. We set ourselves up to be our own authorities, a very dangerous position to be in when relating to God.

Here are six forms of questioning that we need to watch out for. My hope and desire is that each one of us will examine our own hearts and motives when it comes to approaching those in authority over us.

1. Persisting.

This type of questioning attitude is easy to recognize. Once a question is answered the response is, "Let me ask another question." It has as its root a desire to trap the authority figure.

One of our sons, when younger, had a habit of asking questions and then arguing with the answers. If he did not get the answer he wanted to his questions ("Is it okay to go outside?" "May I have another cookie?"), he would respond with "You don't understand" and ask the question again. Oh, on the contrary, we did understand! He had not heard what he wanted to hear and questioned our judgment. He did not really want to hear just any answer; he wanted to hear the answer that coincided with his desires.

One quick note for those who run into a similar pattern with their children. Here is what Joyce and I did. Prior to giving him a response we would ask, "Are you ready for the answer we are going to give, even if it is not what you want to hear?" Sometimes the answer was exactly what he desired while other times it crossed his will. Since we helped him to prepare for the answer, however, his questioning was minimized.

Actually this reminds me of a similar parent/child episode I observed recently. It took place in a grocery store. The daughter wanted to know if she could buy a particular breakfast cereal. The mother said no and explained that it had too much sugar. Instead of accepting the decision of her parent, the daughter launched into a series of questions. "How come Jimmy gets to eat it?" "If I brush my teeth, will it be okay?" "If I buy it with my own money, will it be okay?" Needless to say, the questions continued until a pouting child and frustrated mother stopped talking to one another.

Any number of people—not just children who want their way!—fall into the same pattern. They keep asking the same questions, perhaps changing the wording a bit. No answer will satisfy unless it is the answer they want to hear. They continue to ask until they become wrought with frustration or until those being questioned cave in. Either way, there is an underlying sense of combativeness in their persistent behavior that will surely have an impact on future discussions.

2. Complaining.

This form of questioning is a close relative of *persisting*. We appear to ask a question, but we are really complaining. This form of questioning is similar to a child whining, "Do I have to?" Adults make similar statements, but we are more sophisticated about our whining.

Over the years, when I have disagreed with my supervisors, I have had many excellent discussions with them. Most of the time I was trying to gain further understanding of their approach to the problem at hand. There were times, though, that I simply wanted to convince them that I was right. In questioning their approach I challenged, debated and, yes, complained about anything and everything. These tactics yielded no fruit but the bitter fruit of dissatisfaction.

It is imperative to remember that the responsible leader is in charge and makes the final decision. Usually when we get upset it is because *we* do not have the final say. Keep in mind, if you were the one making the final decision, there would be others (just like us) who would complain about that decision. You may not agree with the boss, but will you submit to the authority of the leader without complaining?

Jesus had to deal constantly with forms of questioning, including "complaining." For instance: "And their scribes and the Pharisees complained against His disciples, saying, 'Why do You eat and drink with tax collectors and sinners?'" (Luke 5:30). It would appear the scribes and Pharisees are not a good combination, frequently ganging up against Jesus. Here they complain about Jesus and His disciples spending time with sinners.

They did not really want an answer from Jesus. No matter what He had said, they would have argued and complained. In fact, this is what happened. He gave them an answer—"I have not come to call the righteous, but sinners, to repentance"—and the scribes and Pharisees came right back with more questioning: "Why do the disciples of John fast often and make prayers, and likewise those of the Pharisees, but Yours eat and drink?" (verse 33). They kept registering specific complaints about His judgment.

3. Challenging.

Questioning that challenges may have its roots in accusation, arrogance or ulterior motives. Jesus was personally confronted over and over again with this type of interaction also. "And the devil said to Him, 'If You are the Son of God, command this stone to become bread'" (Luke 4:3). Satan was challenging Jesus and His authority. The devil did not really want to see a miracle—a stone turned to bread. His posture was questioning and filled with confrontation.

One day many years ago I made an appointment to talk with my pastor because he had made a decision with which I disagreed. My attitude had not improved as I had mulled it over. The more I thought about it, the more I griped about his decision. I did not know everything that had transpired surrounding the decision; all I knew was the final outcome. After several weeks of this inner tirade I made the appointment to "discuss" it.

I sat down in his office and immediately emptied both barrels—one with what I did not like and the other with how I would have handled it differently. After some time of my talking and his listening, he made a pointed observation. "Mike," he said, "it sounds as though you don't trust me." Wow! I had not expected that comment! And I certainly had not planned on checking out my own motives.

The more we talked the more I understood. Yes, he could have made a different decision and he could have taken a different approach with the problem. However, based on all of his information and counsel (which was much broader and deeper than mine), he came to what he saw as the best conclusion. I realized the crux of the matter was indeed, did

I trust my leader? At that moment, I realized I did not. This caused quite a crisis in my life as I had to investigate the source of my mistrust.

In all the years I had known this pastor, he had never done anything to violate my trust. He had not lied to me, had not deceived me and had not lacked integrity in any area of his ministry. In fact, if anything, he was open to other perspectives and was willing to listen—as evidenced by our meeting. So what was it that had led to a feeling of mistrust? My answer was simple yet piercing. I had not gotten my way and therefore felt as though the pastor "just didn't understand." (I guess my son comes by it honestly—or should I say generationally? Gulp!)

This was a valuable lesson for me. I saw that my tendency was to want things done my way, even if I was not in charge—to challenge authority, to question the way things were done instead of learning about the process and trying to understand someone else's reasoning. I was too busy trying to "help" my pastor understand my perspective. Honestly, it was a selfish motive.

When approaching leaders or those in authority, we must examine our motives. In other words, are we interested in hearing their perspectives or are we more interested in sharing our perspectives? Do we want to understand the situations from their viewpoints or do we want them to understand our viewpoints? Do we desire to have an understanding of their thought processes and decision-making or is it more important to point out flaws we perceive in their final analysis?

4. Debating and disputing.

Questioning may take the form of a debate. It may appear initially that you are just asking a question, but before the other person realizes it, you are disputing his authority and asking him to defend himself.

The Pharisees exhibited this behavior as well. In one instance, Jesus was teaching in a home. A paralytic was brought to Him by some friends, but they were unable to get in because of the crowds. So, they climbed up to the roof, pulled their paralyzed friend up by a rope and lowered him down through an opening. When Jesus saw this, He told the paralytic that his sins were forgiven. The scribes and Pharisees were outraged at his audacity to state that He could "take away sins."

> But some of the scribes were sitting there and reasoning in their hearts, "Why does this Man speak blasphemies like this? Who can forgive sins but God alone?" And immediately, when Jesus perceived in His spirit that they reasoned thus within themselves, He said to them, "Why do you reason about these things in your hearts? Which is easier, to say to the paralytic, 'Your sins are forgiven you,' or to say, 'Arise, take up your bed and walk'? But that you may know that the Son of Man has power on earth to forgive sins"—He said to the paralytic, "I say to you, arise, take up your bed, and go your way to your house."
>
> Mark 2:6–11

The man got up and walked out of the house. The Bible states that all were amazed and glorified God. Well, almost all. I am sure that some of the religious people were upset and angry with Jesus for correcting them in front of everyone. As we look closer at this interaction, we can see a clear case of questioning.

Verse eight says, "Jesus perceived in His spirit that they reasoned thus." He knew they were debating with Him in their minds. Jesus responded to them by saying, "Why are you reasoning in your hearts?" The word for *reason* comes from the Greek word *dialogizomal,* which means "to dispute, to deliberate." Jesus was saying, "Why are you disputing with Me? Why are you debating with Me?" The problem was not that their question "Who can forgive sins but God?" was out of line; the problem was that their motive was to dispute Jesus.

I have now presented four motivations for questioning: persisting, complaining, challenging and debating/disputing. Before we continue, take a moment and look at your own life situations. Have you fallen into any of these traps when approaching a person in authority?

5. Making accusations.

An accusing spirit, one that puts people on the defensive, can precede our voices into a conversation. By that I mean that we do not even need to say anything to project an accusatory attitude. Nonverbals like facial expressions and body posture can speak volumes about the thoughts and intents of the heart.

> Now it happened on another Sabbath, also, that He entered the synagogue and taught. And a man was there whose right hand was withered. And the scribes and Pharisees watched Him closely, whether He would heal on the Sabbath, that they might find an accusation against Him. But He knew their thoughts.
>
> Luke 6:6–8

Here once again we have the dynamic duo (or rather the devastating duo) of the scribes and Pharisees waiting for Jesus to do something wrong. If we read on in Luke, we find Jesus telling the man to stretch forth his hand. Jesus then restored the hand "as whole as the other" (Luke 6:10). The Bible states that the scribes and Pharisees "were filled with rage, and discussed with one another what they might do to Jesus" (Luke 6:11).

In this situation, the scribes and Pharisees did not even have to say a word. Jesus knew He was being accused. Have you ever been in a situation where a person did not say a word, but you could tell what he was thinking?

I have a vivid mental picture of my wife walking into one of our sons' rooms and just looking around. Our son, sitting on his bed listening to music, looked up. "Okay, okay. I'll clean up the room" was the quick response to the watchful eye of his mother. Joyce never said a word, but he knew exactly what she was thinking.

The rage expressed by the scribes and Pharisees made it clear something was wrong in their spirits. Yes, we may disagree with someone, but should we be filled with rage? Or do we have an ulterior motive? In the case of the scribes and Pharisees, the motive was clear. They wanted to find something wrong with Jesus so they could bring accusations against Him and destroy Him.

An accusing spirit seeks to destroy. We need to be careful of our suspicious natures and our tendencies to accuse people. Allowing this type of attitude to infiltrate our spirits will pollute us—potentially giving rise to anger and rage, just as it did the Pharisees.

6. Taking up an offense.

A questioning attitude will quickly arise when one is offended. We begin to feel ultra-sensitive and paranoia can overwhelm us. We may sense that others are talking about us, that they do not like us or that they are not being honest with us. This leads us to a feeling of greater offense toward them. The cycle of emotions is repeated, increasing in intensity as it continues.

Now it came to pass, when Jesus finished commanding His twelve disciples, that He departed from there to teach and to preach in their cities. And when John [the Baptist] had heard in prison about the works of Christ, he sent two of his disciples and said to Him, "Are You the Coming One, or do we look for another?"

Matthew 11:1–3

I find this rather an odd question for John to ask Jesus, as it was John himself who foretold of the coming of Jesus and proclaimed Him to be the Messiah. Certainly John knew the answer.

Of even greater interest is the reply that Jesus sent back to John. He told the messengers to let John know that blind eyes now see, lepers are cleansed and the deaf can now hear. Then Jesus added a curious statement: "And blessed is he who is not offended because of Me" (Matthew 11:6). Why did He add that comment? It had nothing to do with the miracles being performed, nor did it speak to Jesus' being the Messiah.

Perhaps it was a subtle message back to John who had been in prison for a while. There is no record of Jesus ever visiting him. I wonder if John was a little piqued that Jesus was pulling "his disciples" away and not recognizing all that John had done. That is speculation, of course, but think about it. Why would John need to ask Jesus if He was the Coming One? John had been so in awe of Jesus, so filled with reverence toward Him, that he had demurred initially about baptizing Him. John knew who Jesus was.

I believe that John was offended. His attitude speaks of questioning Jesus and His authority. Be careful when an offense begins to brew within your heart. A questioning spirit may rise up alongside it.

When we have a questioning attitude toward our bosses, our parents, our pastors, our teachers or any other individuals in a position of authority, it may be due to one of the six aforementioned areas. We must examine our motives and discover what is behind our questioning. While the questions may be legitimate (as were many of the Pharisees' questions), the attitude and spirit behind them may be poisonous.

Asking Questions

Is it ever okay to ask questions of authority figures? Absolutely. Asking questions is healthy and opens up communication. It is a "questioning attitude," shown above, that creates the problem.

When I taught in a junior high school, I had a student in class named Charles. He was challenging, to say the least, but I liked Charles. He had a great sense of humor and was endearing but, yes, his work habits were lacking. Unfortunately, one area not lacking was his temper. One day in another class Charles got in an argument with the teacher. He used inappropriate language and ripped up his textbook in a show of defiance. He was suspended for ten school days.

While I did not condone his actions, I felt I had just begun to reach Charles. His being out of my class for two weeks was not going to help his progress. I understood that one particular teacher was hoping never to see him again, but this punishment was going to have an impact on Charles in my class. So I went to speak with the assistant principal.

I was careful not to criticize or condemn the decision made by the administration. I did not persist in my questions, complain, challenge her authority, debate the issue, make accusations or feel offended. I simply requested that the assistant principal consider how her decision might have ramifications on Charles in his other classes. (I knew that he was doing well in a couple of other classes as well.) I expressed my concern that a two-week suspension would make it very difficult for him to regain his momentum.

I proposed to the administration that Charles not be suspended from my class (or any other class that wanted him). After I shared my perspective, I concluded with, "I appreciate your time and your consideration of my proposal. While I may or may not agree with your final decision, I will support it. It is your decision as the administrator and I am behind you." It was not an attempt to sway her or to gain her favor. I meant every word of it.

When the decision remained to leave him out of school for two weeks, I was fine with it. I would have preferred another course of action, but I felt comfortable with the interaction I had with the assistant principal and I felt her support and appreciation for my forthright approach.

That was not the last time I went to this individual to ask questions. And over the years I found her to be supportive. On numerous occasions she bent over backward to make things work for me. Was the favor I enjoyed due to the way I approached her initially? I think that it weighed heavily into our relationship. Never was I afraid to ask questions, but seldom was I caught in a questioning attitude.

The Bible shares a story about a man named Nicodemus. He was a Pharisee—a learned man—and a ruler of Jews. Some things that Jesus said confused him, but his approach was different from the other Pharisees. Nicodemus simply wanted to ask some questions to gain elucidation and understanding.

> This man came to Jesus by night and said to Him, "Rabbi, we know that You are a teacher come from God; for no one can do these signs that You do unless God is with him." . . . "How can a man be born when he is old? Can he enter a second time into his mother's womb and be born?"
>
> John 3:2, 4

Nicodemus respected Jesus and validated His position and authority. He was not setting Jesus up to be attacked. When Jesus explained that he must be "born of the Spirit," figuratively born again, Nicodemus was still confused so he followed that question with another one: "How can these things be?" (verse 9). He did not condemn Jesus or put Him down. Nicodemus simply said, "I still don't get it." Knowing the man's sincere desire to understand, Jesus continued to explain.

Another example of an appropriate approach to asking questions is found in the gospel of Matthew. Jesus told the parable of the sower. The disciples were confused. "And the disciples came and said to Him, 'Why do You speak to them in parables?'" (Matthew 13:10). Jesus responded to their question by making this statement: "I speak to them in parables, because seeing they do not see, and hearing they do not hear, nor do they understand" (Matthew 13:13). At this point you can bet that they were even more in the dark!

Jesus then proceeded to tell not one more parable, not two, not even three. No, He told four more parables. If ever someone had a reason to be offended, upset or to challenge authority, you would think the disciples did. They had asked a legitimate question and received, so it seemed, more confusion. But look at their motives; they really wanted to understand. They were not looking for an argument or a reason to complain. No one said, "Oh, come on. You're talking foolishness." No. They asked another question—a great question. One that truly showed their desire to learn.

"His disciples came to Him, saying, 'Explain to us the parable of the tares of the field'" (Matthew 13:36). And after Jesus explained it, what did He do? He told three more parables!

Listen, my friends. From time to time we all need to ask questions of authority figures. Asking questions is not the problem; the problem is the attitude behind the questions. Here is a checklist to help you discern your true motives in approaching those in authority.

Checklist for Asking Questions

- Prepare yourself for the discussion. Pray. Ask God to give you words that will be understood. If you feel overly emotional or frustrated, be sure not only to pray but also to receive godly counsel about your upcoming discussion.

Think about what you will say. Write out some thoughts if it will help. Be sure to cover the salient points.

- Find an appropriate time to meet. Avoid quick interactions in the hallway or by the coffeemaker. If the person says, "I only have a few minutes," ask when might be a better time to talk. Be sure to have plenty of time for your discussion. Let the person know how long you might need to meet. If you feel it will take an hour, state this so that the time can be allotted.

- Once you sit down with the person, come to the point. Idle chitchat can help break the ice, but it is better to get started than to have the person wish you would get to the point.

- Follow the procedure Nicodemus followed. Be sure to let the person know that you recognize his or her authority. This is not about trying to prove someone wrong. You desire only to ask a few questions or point out some areas of confusion on your part. The clearer you are about this, the more relaxed and comfortable the person will be with your questions. It will also allow him or her to be open to seeing your point of view. Avoid inflammatory words such as *never, always, you should* (or *shouldn't*) or *if I were you.* These words only create barriers to communication.

- If the explanation you receive still does not clarify the matter for you, follow the example of the disciples. Ask again, outright, for another explanation. "I'm still not sure I get it. Would you please go over that again?" Or "Could you explain it in another way?"

- Be careful not to fall into the trap of becoming defensive. We may start with a question, become defensive and finish by attacking the person. This happens all too often between husbands and wives, parents and children, and among friends.

- Avoid trying to justify yourself and your position. All that needs to be said is, "This is the way I see it" or

"This is the way I am feeling." We may want to justify our reasons for feeling a certain way, but this usually leads to creating excuses. Be sure to give only pertinent examples and not make a laundry list of issues. One or two examples are plenty to give someone the idea.

- When the meeting is concluded, thank the person for his or her time. Ask if you may connect again if further questions arise. (The person might offer that option.)

If the goal is to understand the situation better and to express our concerns, communication will take place. If the goal is to prove our points or to get the person to admit his or her mistakes, plan on a long, arduous meeting.

One last point to mention here. Suppose you have shared your concerns and your advice was not heeded. Then later it becomes obvious that you were right. In such a case, avoid the "I told you so" remarks. They are destructive.

Imagine Jesus, after being denied by Peter, turning and saying, "I told you so." Or how about Noah, while the rain poured down, shouting down to the people on the ground, "You should have listened to me." Absurd?

I have often wondered if the disciples discerned things about Judas. They were all together for a few years. Could you not imagine that the disciples sensed a spirit of betrayal in Judas? Perhaps they noticed him taking money from the treasury or heard him whisper negative comments about Jesus to other people. Might not Matthew have turned to James and said, "I just saw Judas talking to the chief priests. That's kind of weird." Maybe someone even spoke to Jesus and expressed concerns. I think that they must have seen things, heard things, felt things they conveyed to Jesus. Yet Jesus continued to have Judas in His midst.

When Judas finally betrayed Jesus, I wonder if anyone thought, *I knew it. I never felt good about him.* Or, *I tried to warn the Master. Nobody ever listens to me.* Jesus knew about Judas all the time. Was He waiting for a heart change in Judas?

Was He hoping for repentance and restoration? I do not know the answer to that, but it is important to remember that your heart attitude will likely be revealed at some point. The fact that people might not agree with you is no reason to think that they are not aware of what you are thinking.

If there were any complaints from the disciples, Jesus chose to ignore them and go another direction. We must be careful with our attitudes when situations do not turn out the way that we would prefer. It is important to share our perspectives, but we must never try to force our plans on others, especially on our authorities.

Personally, I am grateful for the mercy shown me by my leaders, authorities and supervisors over the years. After any number of my flops one of them could have said, "I knew Mike would blow it. I told you so." Instead, they encouraged me, believed in me and trusted that I would humble myself and receive guidance and counsel in order to learn from my mistakes.

One Final Thought . . .

It is good to ask questions, especially when we are uncertain, unsure or confused. However, we must check our attitudes and be certain that we do not fall into a position of "questioning." Questioning will only yield mistrust and division. Our motives should be to bring greater understanding and clarity to situations. Should we speak up or should we be silent? We must consider our choices prayerfully.

1. Think of a time when you approached someone with a "questioning" attitude. How did he or she respond to you?
2. What about a time when you approached someone with a pure attitude of asking questions? Was the response different?

six

The Code
of Silence

The most important thought to enter my mind is my individual responsibility to God.

Daniel Webster

"We are in this together. Let's make a pact not to tell anyone." These words have been spoken innumerable times throughout history. From Abraham and his deceit regarding his true relationship with Sarah to Judas Iscariot making a deal with the chief priests, the Bible clearly illustrates the temptation to gain advantage through deceitfulness. What coerced Joseph's brothers to try to destroy Joseph and then hide their deed? What pressured Ananias and Sapphira, people of integrity, to lie to the apostle Peter? The enticement to be secretive, to be devious and to withhold information is a battle for many of us. In this chapter, we will examine possible motivations for our dishonesty. We will view the power of peer influence and ways to overcome the pressure we may feel to be a part of a code of silence.

In the Beginning

It does not take long to find a biblical pattern of deceit among men: Yes, we have a sinful nature, a fallen nature that usually leads us toward dishonesty and guile. This is why it seems at times as though it is easier to be deceptive than honest. Let's investigate numerous examples illustrated in the Bible that set a foundation for our understanding of deceit.

> And they heard the sound of the LORD God walking in the garden in the cool of the day, and Adam and his wife hid themselves from the presence of the LORD God among the trees of the garden.
>
> Genesis 3:8

Adam and Eve refused to be honest and confront their mistake in disobeying the command of God. This is the first recorded incident in which people agree to remain silent even though it conceals the truth. To this day, we still attempt to hide from God, hoping He will not find us and see our mistakes.

> Then the LORD said to Cain, "Where is Abel your brother?" And he said, "I do not know. Am I my brother's keeper?"
>
> Genesis 4:9

Cain killed Abel out of jealousy and then hoped no one would notice Abel was gone. Honestly, it was not as though he could get lost in a crowd! Lying and deceit distort our perspectives and create false perceptions of life.

> "Please say you are my sister, that it may be well with me for your sake, and that I may live because of you."
>
> Genesis 12:13

Abram was fearful that Pharaoh would see his beautiful wife, Sarai, and kill him in order to take her into Pharaoh's own household. (Remember that this is just before the point in history when God renamed Abraham and Sarah.) They conspired to lie about their true husband-and-wife relationship and she was indeed taken to Pharaoh's house. God intervened and Pharaoh sent them away.

They continued in their journey and stayed in a place called Gerar.

> Now Abraham said of Sarah his wife, "She is my sister." And Abimelech king of Gerar sent and took Sarah.
>
> Genesis 20:2

Here we go again. God had just made a covenant with Abraham, foretold of Abraham's descendants and the multiplication of nations, and promised that Abraham and Sarah would have a son, but Abraham lied once more, choosing deceit over trust in God. Abraham and Sarah schemed to hide behind their lie and to keep silent about the truth.

> And it came to pass, when Jezebel heard that Naboth had been stoned and was dead, that Jezebel said to Ahab, "Arise, take possession of the vineyard of Naboth the Jezreelite, which he refused to give you for money; for Naboth is not alive, but dead."
>
> 1 Kings 21:15

Ahab desired the vineyard next to the palace. He offered to buy it from Naboth, the owner, but was refused. Jezebel used an evil report, a vicious rumor to destroy Naboth's reputation and had him killed. Together, Ahab and Jezebel possessed the vineyard and the land. They agreed to a code of silence and to hide behind a façade of deceit.

Then [Haman's] wife Zeresh and all his friends said to him, "Let a gallows be made, fifty cubits high, and in the morning suggest to the king that Mordecai be hanged on it; then go merrily with the king to the banquet." And the thing pleased Haman; so he had the gallows made.

Esther 5:14

Haman hated Mordecai because he had refused to "bow down and tremble" before him. The plan was to kill Mordecai by hanging him from the gallows. Unfortunately for Haman and his family, it was Haman who was hanged on that very gallows. God was, and is, faithful to those who honor Him.

Trickery, lies and dishonesty are not traits found only in the Old Testament. The "new covenant" did not destroy the tendency of people to want to manipulate a situation for their own gain. We do now have a Counselor, the Holy Spirit, who can help guide and focus our intentions if we so choose or we can decide to listen to our own voices, voices that usually bend toward selfishness and self-interest.

Then the chief priests, the scribes, and the elders of the people assembled at the palace of the high priest, who was called Caiaphas, and plotted to take Jesus by trickery and kill Him.

Matthew 26:3–4

The tendency to hide, to plot and to be deceitful was still intact thousands of years after Adam and Eve. The characters and names were different, but the words and actions were the same: "Let's keep it to ourselves. It's our little secret." How many lives have been destroyed and destinies derailed because of these little secrets?

But a certain man named Ananias, with Sapphira his wife, sold a possession. And he kept back part of the proceeds, his wife also being aware of it, and brought a certain part and laid it at the apostles' feet.

Acts 5:1–2

The result of this action was the death of both Ananias and Sapphira. They were struck dead—not because they held back money for their own use but because they lied about it and were deceitful to God. Many spiritual deaths have occurred due to dishonesty. Many times the dishonesty stems from an agreement of silence among friends, family or spiritual brothers and sisters.

And when it was day, some of the Jews banded together and bound themselves under an oath, saying that they would neither eat nor drink till they had killed Paul.

Acts 23:12

Here we have a large group of people who conspired to destroy Paul. This agreement, this covenant with one another was cloaked in secrecy. If a secret is meant to harm another person, it is a fair assumption that it is not of God. By the way, either they all died from starvation or they broke their oath because this group was not responsible for Paul's death.

Trapped by Rationalizing

The propensity toward self-protection, selfishness and self-preservation is a constant theme in the lives of many people throughout the Scriptures. Likewise, this code of silence is found within the lives of many people today.

I am presently in the midst of working with two neighbors who have become offended with one another. Terry borrowed a lawnmower from Shane. The mower broke. Terry refuses to fix it, saying it was already defective. It is apparent from our conversations that this is just a smokescreen. The real issue is the fact that Terry does not have enough money to pay for the repairs. He is justifying his position by insisting that the mower was old and would have broken down soon.

Unfortunately, instead of being honest, as he has been encouraged to be, he has built up a wall of excuses and blame toward Shane. Terry claims that Shane has not returned some of his tools, therefore he is under no obligation to fix the broken lawnmower. Is this beginning to sound like a soap opera? Terry refuses to be honest with Shane and discuss his financial situation. Their anger has grown to the point that they refuse to speak to one another. They attend the same church but find it uncomfortable to see one another in social settings.

Terry is now refusing to go to church. He will not return phone calls from friends and has expressed his conviction that everyone is against him. He has become bitter to the point of isolation.

Dishonesty, trickery, deceit, lying—each may be justified in our own minds. We rationalize and develop our own sense of morality in order to protect ourselves. Unfortunately a web of deceit usually ends up creating more problems than originally existed. "All the ways of a man are pure in his own eyes, but the LORD weighs the spirits [or motives]" (Proverbs 16:2).

Sometimes speaking up is not easy, but the alternatives can be devastating. Is there a way to break out of the trap of rationalizing and justifying our actions? When we allow anger, bitterness and resentment to constrict our emotions and thoughts, self-protection kicks into action. Try a few of the following ideas the next time a "cycle of rationalization" traps you into silence.

1. *If you find yourself thinking "I was right, wasn't I?" you probably need to take a step back.* If you are questioning your own decisions, it may be helpful to get another opinion instead of getting upset. Becoming angry is neither right nor wrong. It is the manner in which we put our anger into action that creates the problem. People who seek justification for their behavior

are often attempting to rationalize or excuse their own anger and the consequences of their imprudent action.

2. *Lose the need to be in control.* We cannot control everything. (Although I do try from time to time.) Too often we feel the urge to "help" others change their lives, their attitudes and their actions. I have a hard enough time trying to take care of me and others placed in my care without worrying about the world at large. Remember the words of the Serenity Prayer:

> God grant me the serenity
> to accept the things I cannot change;
> courage to change the things I can;
> and wisdom to know the difference.

It is called the Serenity Prayer for a reason. We will understand a great deal about speaking up and remaining silent if we can apprehend the wisdom in this simple prayer.

3. *Forgive and heal when you have been hurt.* We like to say "forgive and forget," but that is oftentimes very difficult. Instead, we need to heal. It is okay if mistakes are made and errors take place. The key is having the grace and willingness to forgive others. Then when we remember the hurt, we can avoid falling into the pattern of anger and resentment. We must step back and accept responsibility for our own involvement while releasing a prayer of forgiveness over the others involved. It is difficult, but it does become easier the more we put it into practice.

4. *Do not take the blame for life's problems, and avoid placing the blame on others.* Examine the cause of the problem. If it is due to something that can be corrected or improved upon—such as your communication, attention or sensitivity—address those areas squarely. If, however, the cause is beyond your control—the way another person acts, lack of resources, circumstances—avoid the frustration of asking "What if?" or "Why?" Those questions can never be answered and they deplete our emotional resources unnecessarily.

5. *If you find it too difficult to pull out of the blame game or the rationalization cycle, talk to someone whom you trust and respect.* Explain the cyclical patterns you have established in life. Stay accountable to that person. Be honest about your patterns and difficulties. Allow him or her to guide you and counsel you through situations that come up. This may be necessary until you begin to see things more clearly.

6. *Communicate your feelings and concerns in a way that can be received by the other person.* I recently sent a letter that, I regret to say, had an "edge" to it. The recipient was upset with me for being too blunt. In retrospect, I realized that he was correct and I asked for his forgiveness. The point I wanted to get across was important and the issue was appropriate, but in my frustration I rationalized an approach that only alienated him further. I spent a week trying to clean up my mess, one that should never have occurred.

Facing Pressure

There are those who, despite their best intentions, have found themselves caught in prickly situations because of peer pressure and unfortunate circumstances. These can be times when a group of friends want to go someplace you do not, or when several family members decide to watch something on television you are not comfortable watching. It may be a conversation you wish would stop or the way your group is acting toward another individual. Once several people have come into agreement, it is difficult to find the words that could break the momentum gained by their focused direction. Peer pressure is a powerful force.

One of the most profound biblical examples of pressure to join together in a code of silence is the story of Joseph and his eleven brothers told in the book of Genesis. Though Joseph was eventually sold into slavery, his brothers originally intended to kill him. Or, rather, almost all his brothers. There was one who attempted to disagree with the mob of men whispering, "Death to the dreamer, our brother." There was one who was willing to take a stand and save his life. And yet, even this bold individual caved in to some degree.

The Bible states that "[Jacob] loved Joseph more than all his children" (Genesis 37:3). Certainly this would create a jealousy among siblings. Years ago, there was a comedy team called the Smothers Brothers. Younger brother Tommy would always say to older brother Dick, "Mom always liked you best." He would then use several humorous examples of her favoritism. "You always get more candles on your cake than I do." "Mom gave you the keys to the car before me."

"Mom [or Dad] always liked you best" is not an uncommon feeling in a family with more than one child. Each one may feel that the parent(s) show preferential treatment to another sibling. This may cause friction and jealousy.

In the case of Joseph and his brothers, the issue was compounded when Jacob gave Joseph a colored tunic. This "coat of many colors" should rightfully have been given to the oldest son, Reuben. It was part of the heritage and inheritance of the eldest in the family. Reuben, however, had violated his father's trust and the morality of the law of Israel. He had slept with Bilhah, one of his father's concubines (see Genesis 35:21–22). It is probably due to this sin in Reuben's life that Jacob chose to withhold this blessing from him. The whispers of jealousy and hatred spread quickly and constantly among the brothers. "When his brothers saw that their father loved [Joseph] more than all his brothers, they hated him and could not speak peaceably to him" (Genesis 37:4).

Then, as if he were not alienated enough from the family, seventeen-year-old Joseph was given dreams from God about them. In one dream Joseph's brothers, symbolized by sheaves, bowed down to him. A subsequent dream illustrated Joseph's brothers, father and mother bowing down to him. This was too much for the brothers who now openly envied and hated Joseph. Feelings of contempt churned within the brothers at his audacity. *Who does he think he is? Dreams from God? Indeed!*

We might ask whether or not this was a time for Joseph to be silent and keep the dreams to himself. Perhaps. What was his purpose in sharing his dreams with his family? Conceit? Arrogance? Boasting? We really do not know, but we have no record that God directed Joseph to repeat them. So let me give you a little counsel. If you have dreams or visions of your family bowing down to you, get some counsel before you share them.

One day the brothers were feeding their flock of sheep in nearby Shechem. Jacob suggested Joseph go and see how his brothers fared. Without hesitation, Joseph set out to find them. When they saw Joseph coming, anger rose up in them. The impudence and arrogance of their younger brother in proclaiming his lordship over them stirred in their memories. The closer Joseph came, the more infuriated they grew. A plan of destruction began to crystallize in their minds.

"Come therefore, let us now kill him and cast him into some pit; and we shall say, 'Some wild beast has devoured him.' We shall see what will become of his dreams!" (Genesis 37:20). The brothers agreed to this plan—all but one, that is.

We usually hear that "all" the brothers wanted to kill Joseph, but that is not the case. Reuben heard the scheme and rose up to protect his little brother. As the "oldest brother," Reuben may have felt protective of the family, even of Joseph the dreamer. Though possibly offended at Joseph's attitude and proclamation of future greatness, Reuben held fast to his desire to protect his family. "But Reuben heard it, and he delivered him out of their hands, and said, 'Let us not kill him.' And Reuben said to them, 'Shed no blood, but cast him into this pit which is in the wilderness, and do not lay a hand on him'—that he might deliver him out of their hands, and bring him back to his father" (Genesis 37:21–22).

This was an interesting situation. It appears that the plan to kill Joseph was impromptu, devised on the spur of the moment, but Reuben would not go along with it. This is especially significant because he was the one brother who might have had a valid reason to be jealous and angry with Joseph. After all, Joseph did receive the blessing of the "colored coat" that normally would have been bestowed upon the eldest son. Reuben did not take the bait of the enemy and give in to the crowd mentality. While the others were plotting to kill Joseph, Reuben took a stand for righteousness.

The brothers cast Joseph into a pit without food or water as they discussed his fate. They sat down to a meal and looked up to see a group of Ishmaelite traders headed for Egypt. Judah turned to the brothers and suggested they sell Joseph and at least make some money. Unfortunately for Joseph, Reuben was not around. Whether Reuben was checking on the sheep, taking a walk to develop his own strategy to release Joseph or even asleep is unknown. However, due to Reuben's absence, the brothers were able to sell Joseph into slavery.

Later, Reuben returned intending to get Joseph out of the pit, but Joseph was already gone. Greatly distressed, Reuben tore his clothes, which represented mourning and sorrow. As a point of closure and perhaps explanation of Joseph's absence, the brothers smeared blood on Joseph's tunic and showed it to their father who concluded that some wild animal had torn poor Joseph to shreds.

Reuben had a choice to make at this point—either enter the code of silence with his brothers or speak up and risk their wrath and fury. His courage failed. He should have stood up for his convictions and told his father what had happened, but his silence made him part and parcel of the deception to make his father believe that Joseph was dead.

To go along with the group or step out and make an independent decision, an unpopular one at that, was a tough decision indeed. Of course, as we continue to read the story of Joseph we see God's sovereign hand at work. Years later Joseph told his brothers, "You meant evil against me; but God meant it for good, in order to bring it about as it is this day, to save many people alive" (Genesis 50:20).

Each one of us has found ourselves in a place where, like Reuben, we need to decide either to succumb to the pressure of the majority or to vocalize a different perspective. Too often we take a stand for what we believe only to fall back when the opposition seems too great.

Was it peer pressure that allowed 250 leaders to gather with Korah against Moses? Was it peer pressure (and fear) that prevented anyone except Nathan from confronting King David regarding his sins of adultery with Bathsheba and the murder of Uriah? Certainly we could say that peer pressure was a significant factor in Peter's denial of Jesus.

How do we handle the pressure to join in a code of silence? Below are some suggestions that may help next time you are feeling the weight of group influence.

Surviving Peer Pressure

Here are five strategies to help you withstand pressure. These are great to teach children as well.

1. Ask questions. Asking questions puts you in a place of power and puts the other person on the defensive. Questions can cause the other person to back down from being so pushy. The more appropriate questions you ask, the more the other person realizes you will not be easily swayed.

"What movie did you say we are going to see?" is a question that will help you avoid getting surprised by a stronger rating than you would prefer.

"I know you all want to go out drinking, but what do you think our parents would say if they found out? I'm underage. Anybody here of a legal age to drink?"

"Yes, I could lie to the boss about what happened today. But if I do, will she trust me in future situations?"

2. Be aware of your pressure zones. Where do you receive most of the pressure? Is it with certain people? At work? With family? It is imperative to know the areas where the pressure is especially strong. In college I had a friend named Dave. We would go out and "party" quite heavily. After I became a Christian I felt tremendous pressure from him to get back into the drinking and drug scene. One night I went out drinking with him. Though I had expressed mild resistance to doing so, I allowed him to convince me that it would be like old times. The next day I was filled with conviction. I was embarrassed by my inability to stand up to Dave and hold fast to my beliefs. Recognizing my weakness, I decided to reduce my contact with Dave until I could be stronger about my personal convictions.

3. *Use the buddy system.* It is easier to say no and avoid pressure when someone else supports you. The disciples were sent in pairs, not alone. It was important for them to get support and strength from one another. Whether at work or in a family situation, attempt to find at least one other person who will support you. If necessary, call a friend and have him pray for you before entering into a "pressure zone." Be accountable and tell him you will call when you get back and describe what happened. This will help you feel emotional support even in your friend's physical absence.

4. *Say no as though you mean it.* Do not mumble, act apologetic or be wishy-washy with your decisions. Maintain eye contact. Be forceful. Be certain of your answers and let others know your decisions are final. You do not need to yell or argue. Use the broken-record approach. Repeat your answers several times. "No, I'm not interested." "No, I don't want to do that." Think back to the story of Joseph. Reuben was strong initially, but he wavered and then compromised by having Joseph thrown in the pit. Instead of taking a strong stand—"We will not hurt our brother. Leave him alone"—Reuben relented and then tried to sneak back and save Joseph. This type of backdoor approach usually fails to get the point across.

5. *Evaluate your friendships.* Miguel de Cervantes, author of *Don Quixote* and other works, writes: "Tell me what company you keep, and I'll tell you who you are." Do your friends

support you and your dreams, ambitions, desires? Are they willing to challenge you and give guidance and counsel about your decisions? We all need people who will stand up for us and support our individuality, but not stand by and let us make poor choices. A friend will challenge us, confront us and encourage us not to make decisions without godly guidance.

While these five steps alone may not always prevent us from bowing down to pressure, they will help each one of us to be more confident of our own personal perspectives, values and beliefs.

One Final Thought . . .

We will face frequent opportunities to "join in" criticism or to "fall into" agreement with plans contrary to our own beliefs. We all want to have friends and to be considered part of the group, but at what cost? Are we willing to set ourselves apart for the sake of our own convictions? Compromising our own values and beliefs must become more difficult than assenting to the pressure from others. Our voices must arise when we sense a need to take a stand.

1. Can you remember the last time you justified an action? What was the underlying reason?
2. When you feel pressure from others to make decisions, how have you typically responded? What would help you respond differently?

seven

The Purpose of Silence

Silence is safer than speech.

Epictetus, Greek philosopher

To this point, we have discussed how silence can be a barrier to communication. Being silent may allow someone else to make a painful mistake or choose an avoidable decision. A strong case has been made as to the importance of speaking up and having a voice in situations. But we also know that the Bible calls for "a time for silence."

Indeed, there are times we should be silent because it is best for the situation. We may feel a prodding of the Holy Spirit to hold our tongue and allow for God's divine intervention. There may be others who need to speak instead of us—some who may have greater insights or knowledge. And yes, there may be times when speaking creates a greater problem.

In this chapter, we will explore times to be silent. How will we know if we should speak or hold our peace? The Bible is full of illustrations of God-directed silence for, naturally, God directs times of silence just as He directs us to speak. We do not always find this easy to follow. We want to speak, to make a case for our way of thinking. Let's begin by looking at some of the hindrances to remaining silent.

Stumbling Blocks

Through nine different plagues—miracles from God—Moses pursued freedom for the Israelites. God had sent Moses to be a voice, to confront Pharaoh. And then, after nine catastrophic plagues, Moses had to make a decision between silence and continuing his open assault upon Pharaoh.

> Then Pharaoh said to [Moses], "Get away from me! Take heed to yourself and see my face no more! For in the day you see my face you shall die!" And Moses said, "You have spoken well. I will never see your face again."
>
> Exodus 10:28–29

Moses discerned here that silence was the correct response. Pharaoh's heart was hardened and no pleading, threats, persuading or discussion would change his mind. If Moses had argued with Pharaoh or come against him at this juncture, he would have been operating within his own strength while the release of the Hebrew people hung in the balance.

The first potential stumbling block to God-inspired silence is *feeling threatened or intimidated*. When someone threatens us or tries to bully us, it is not uncommon to want to fight back. If we feel picked on or persecuted, our response may be one of aggression. It is critical for us to be "slow to speak, slow to wrath" (James 1:19).

When growing up in Arizona I remember seeing several schoolyard fights. (And yes, sometimes I saw them a little too closely.) During these fights, it was typical to see one kid bullying another. The aggressor tried to badger the other into a fight. If the intended victim chose to remain silent, he usually was able to remove himself unscathed from the scene. If, however, the intended victim chose to fight back verbally, a physical fight ensued.

People who use intimidation and threats are counting on the other person to respond. It is through the response that further venom can be spewed forth by the antagonist. Just as any further discussion by Moses would have increased Pharaoh's hatred, so we find ourselves in situations where our voices could create further problems. Be careful to avoid getting trapped by intimidation or threats.

Fear is the second stumbling block to maintaining a godly silence. If we are afraid, we may find ourselves talking unwisely. You probably have heard this in public speakers. They begin to speak more quickly or their thought processes appear flighty or they begin to ask numerous questions in order to ease their fears.

The familiar story of Abraham's taking Isaac to the mountain is a wonderful example of the peace of God overcoming fear. Abraham was given a "faith" task—to take his son to the mountains and sacrifice him to God (see Genesis 22). Sacrificing children to gods was a heathen practice, but Abraham did not question God. Abraham knew his God and was willing to proceed in faith. And what of Isaac? When he was told there would be a sacrifice, but no lamb was brought forth, he could have asked many questions but none are recorded. When he was bound with rope may have been a good time to ask questions. And when Abraham laid his son on the altar of wood and brought out a knife, certainly the fear must have been overwhelming for both of them. Would Abraham or Isaac break the silence?

Isaac trusted his father and was confident that all would be fine. His internal security regarding his father, his God and his future was greater than his external insecurity. When we feel the peace of God and have a certainty of who we are in Christ, we lose interest in trying to justify ourselves or trying to fit every piece of life's puzzles into our human framework.

Certainly, we are not to keep our mouths shut when something happens to cause us discomfort. Or are we? In the above illustration there is no biblical mention of Isaac being afraid. In fact, Abraham may have been more anxious than his son. The key is to be sure fear does not grip you and pressure you toward needing the comfort of words. We must learn to find the comfort of silence.

A third area that may lead us to forsake godly silence is *pride.* We like to brag about our accomplishments and our achievements. We have a desire for personal recognition: We want someone to know that the idea was ours, that we are the leaders, that we are special. Our own egos can lead us to ruin the purpose of silence.

> And they [the shepherds] came with haste and found Mary and Joseph, and the Babe lying in a manger. Now when they had seen Him, they made widely known the saying which was told them concerning this Child. And all those who heard it marveled at those things which were told them by the shepherds. But Mary *kept all these things and pondered them in her heart.*
>
> Luke 2:16–19, emphasis added

Imagine: "My son, the Messiah!" Yet the response by His mother was to ponder it in her heart. Wow! Honestly, how many of us would be on the phone to the local paper, television show or national magazine? This is a *news* story. Why were Mary and Joseph not jumping up and down shouting, "Guess what? Our son is the *Messiah*"? If one of my sons hits a home run, does well on a test or even cleans up his room, it is big news.

In the days to come, both Simeon, a devout Jew, and Anna, a prophetess, spoke words of revelation, destiny and calling over Jesus. Again, Joseph and Mary kept this to themselves, contemplated the significance, measured and weighed the cost and burden of such an issue. Silence was in order. They knew the truth and did not need to convince anyone else. Pride was stifled as the confidence and comfort of silence emerged.

Silence may allow the truth to come forth on its own. Not long ago, I met with a young man who confessed to me about a dishonest business dealing with a friend. He had lied to his friend about the price of an item in order to make a larger profit. His friend found out and their relationship was fractured. The young man was not repentant; rather, he rationalized what he had done. As he told his story, I asked a few questions and clarified a few points, but I did not challenge his apparent transgressions. There are appropriate times to confront sin, but I sensed that this was not one of them. Until God reached through to his heart, my words would have little impact. I told him I would pray for their relationship to be restored and believed that in the near future, he would have a greater sense of understanding and direction. I also asked him to think about how his friend perceived his placing money at a greater premium than their friendship.

A week or two later, this young man grabbed me after a church meeting. He told me he had gone back to his friend and repented for lying. He acknowledged the deceit and asked his friend to keep him more accountable in his business dealings. I had helped him process his thinking without confronting the sin, and my silence allowed time for God to deal with the situation.

While threats, fear and pride are not the only reasons silence is broken, they are among the most common. When you are in a situation and one of these areas becomes evident, take a deep breath, pray an extra prayer and be sure you are not "bullied" to speak out. Your silence will probably be of greater impact than an emotional outburst.

Does this mean that we can just be silent in any conflict and thereby remain innocent of any guilt? If you answered yes, review the story of Adam and Eve. To help evaluate our motivation for silence, it may be helpful to ask ourselves a few questions:

1. Why was I silent?
2. Did God's Spirit or my flesh motivate my silence?
3. Was the silence helpful in furthering God's Kingdom, in clarifying the issues, in allowing a person to gain greater insights into his or her own life?
4. After my silence, did I second-guess myself?
5. Did I suppress an urging to speak? If so, why did I suppress it?

Hearing the Voice of God

The supreme comfort of peace is found within Jesus Christ. He was betrayed, arrested, bound, mocked, falsely accused, physically attacked and badgered by questions, yet He did not strike back with words.

> Now Jesus stood before the governor. And the governor asked Him, saying, "Are You the King of the Jews?" So Jesus said to him, "It is as you say." And while He was being accused by the chief priests and elders, He answered nothing. Then Pilate said to Him, "Do You not hear how many things they testify against You?" And He answered him not one word, so that the governor marveled greatly.
>
> Matthew 27:11–14

Do you see that at this point anything Jesus said would have been twisted, turned and rejected? We have talked about being sure our attitudes are correct before we speak. We investigated the importance of having a proper spirit and proper motivation when confronting. Unfortunately, there are times when no matter how right a spirit you have and no matter how positive your attitude may be, others will respond with anger, mockery or indifference. (We will talk more specifically about facing anger in the next chapter.)

Jesus understood silence. Why defend? Why justify? Why try to explain when someone's mind is made up? He knew only a sovereign touch from God could change their minds. Parents, children, leaders, employees, supervisors, pastors, are you listening? There is a time to be silent. It can bring comfort and inner peace when God has directed it.

We can recognize that peaceful silence. It is felt when dad and mom get all their children to bed at night and they just sit and rest. Or when after a hectic day the supervisor sits out on the deck or porch watching a sunset. We experience this stillness in God during prayer or during a worshipful time with our Lord. We must also learn to find this tranquility of godly silence within the context of our busy lives.

Silence in Action

Lloyd, one of the custodians at an agency where I worked, was a young man who had mastered this. His crew would usually arrive at around five P.M. just as we were closing. There were times I worked late and I observed his genuine concern for the details of his job. I enjoyed his enthusiasm as well as his excellent work ethic.

In fact, all of us at the agency appreciated the great care Lloyd took in dusting each desk, polishing the wood floor in the hallway and cleaning the glass in the foyer. The garbage was not just emptied; he made sure that the can was clean before placing another liner carefully inside. When he vacuumed the floors, he did not leave a trace of paper or lint. He demanded this type of attentiveness from his two employees as well.

In addition, Lloyd had a great sense of humor. His laughter would fill a room and create an ambiance of joy. Our Christmas parties and other gatherings were always more festive when Lloyd was a part of them.

I entered work one morning and my boss pulled me aside. "Did you hear about Lloyd?" she asked. I had not. She proceeded to tell me the story.

One of my coworkers, Nancy, was missing a significant amount of cash from her desk drawer. Nancy was getting ready to take a trip and had gone to the bank. Foolishly, she had gotten about a thousand dollars in cash and put it in her desk. The next day, her cash was gone. She stated that she had a late-afternoon appointment out of the office that day and had planned to come back and get the money. She said that she became ill and could not return until the next morning. The money was gone.

Since Lloyd and his crew were the only ones who were in the office after hours, it was a natural assumption that one of them took the money. Since Lloyd was responsible for cleaning Nancy's office, suspicion fell on him. When questioned, however, Lloyd refused to say much more than, "I didn't do it."

As each day passed and the investigation intensified, Lloyd continued to respond to the accusations with the simple, emphatic statement "I didn't do it. I am innocent." We all found this rather odd, assuming that an innocent man would surely make vociferous and numerous protests in such a situation.

At the end of the week one of the other custodians, a member of his work crew named Ben, came forward, admitted taking the money and returned it to Nancy. Lloyd was completely exonerated.

I found it curious that Lloyd never spoke up in his defense. So one day, about a month or so later, I was working late and saw Lloyd being his usual proficient self. I asked him if he had a few minutes. We sat in my office and after a few moments I asked him a direct question. "Lloyd," I said, "help me out. When you were accused of stealing, you did very little to protect yourself. You barely issued a denial. Did you know that Ben had taken the money?"

"I had my suspicions. He helped me clean the office that night and acted rather oddly the rest of the evening."

This only aroused my curiosity further. "Why didn't you tell this to the police?" I asked. His response taught me a lot about the power of silence.

"After the police left, I sat down with Ben and Victor [his other employee]. I told them I had not taken the money and knew it was one of them. I also said that I was not planning on telling the police but expected the one who took the money to come forward on his own." He looked at me with a wry smile and added, "They had worked with me for many years and knew I was committed to them. I believed that whoever was guilty would be convicted by his own conscience, particularly when seeing me accused of something I had not done."

"But what if Ben never admitted it?"

"Then," he said, "I felt confident that my innocence would overshadow the apparent guilt. I believe that God will bring light to the darkness. I didn't need to 'prove' my innocence. I was already innocent."

He left the room and I sat still, pondering his wisdom and his approach. To this day I am amazed at his response. I am not sure that I totally understand his trust in his employees or his ability to stay quiet, but I do understand his faith—a belief that righteousness will overshadow unrighteousness, that innocence will prevail over guilt and that truth will eventually be found. I am grateful that for Lloyd it happened sooner than later.

There are those who are not as fortunate. Their faith is firm, they have the same peace and comfort as Lloyd, but they must wait much longer than a week for their names to be cleared and for restoration to take place. Yet they continue in peace. How is this possible?

Think, too, of the apostle Paul and the suffering he endured during his life. He was beaten, imprisoned, persecuted and mocked for his beliefs. At times he spoke out and shared his convictions with others. At other times he was separated and isolated, yet his strength and fortitude never wavered. How was Paul able to maintain his love for people, his desire to see restoration in the Church? I have drawn several key factors from people like Lloyd and the apostle Paul that are necessary if we are to make effective use of silence:

- If the sense you have to remain silent lines up with the Word of God.
- If biblically based counsel from spiritual leaders confirms it.
- If you have prayed and your decision is confirmed by two or more witnesses to the situation.
- If you have peace in your spirit. (God always brings peace, *not* stress.)

However (there is always a "however"), remember that silence can also be used as an excuse to comfort our flesh, to protect us from involvement and to rationalize inactivity. Let's review quickly two Bible stories where silence was used to comfort the flesh and not further the Kingdom.

One of the greatest accounts of a spiritual battle is recorded in 1 Kings. It is the story of Elijah standing against the 450 false prophets who served the king and queen in Israel. Elijah was neither intimidated nor fearful. He challenged them to a dual, a spiritual championship. He withstood their attempts to call upon their god, Baal, and then watched as God responded to his prayer by calling down fire from heaven. What a scene!

Then one person threatened his life and his bravery flew out the window. Queen Jezebel, in a fit of rage, sent this message to Elijah: "So let the gods do to me, and more also, if I do not make your life as the life of one of them by tomorrow about this time" (1 Kings 19:2). The Bible says that when he heard this, he arose in fear and ran for his life. Where was the faith, the confidence to challenge, to stand up for what was right? Jezebel's words put fear into Elijah and effectively silenced the prophet's voice. His flesh was comforted by his escape, but his spirit had no peace.

Now look at an example involving the disciples. I believe we can all agree that the disciples were typically not concerned about talking too much. Silence was not their problem. If they had questions, they were all bold about expressing them. But when Jesus warned the disciples of the impending betrayal at the hands of men, there was an unusual response (or rather lack of response).

> He said to His disciples, "Let these words sink down into your ears, for the Son of Man is about to be betrayed into the hands of men." But they did not understand this saying, and it was hidden from them so that they did not perceive it; and they were afraid to ask Him about this saying.
>
> Luke 9:43–45

Afraid? Since when? Were they fearful they would be implicated? If anything, it seems that they would have asked Jesus to explain what He meant or would have seen if there was some way to protect Him. Again we see that silence— when used to comfort the flesh, to avoid possible confrontations or challenges—is not necessarily inspired by God.

One Final Thought . . .

We have seen how silence can mean comfort from God or comfort for our flesh. If it is from God, revelation may break forth. The individual may grow in wisdom and knowledge regarding his or her life situation. Typically bondage is broken when godly silence prevails. But if God has directed us to speak and we remain silent, we stay petrified, bound, chained and unable to move toward freedom. Silence: from God or from the flesh? It is a question that must be answered in each situation.

1. Besides threats, fear and pride, are there other reasons you have not been silent?
2. How do you know when God is telling you to be silent? List several ways you know.

eight

Walking in Peace

I am very little inclined on any occasion to say anything unless I hope to produce some good by it.

Abraham Lincoln

Have you ever been accused of something, known your innocence, but said nothing? As you remained silent the lies and distortions only increased. Yet you knew vindication would come when it was time. You held your comments, knowing that your words would only inflame the issue. It takes confidence and faith that the truth will come forth to do this.

We will focus in this chapter on those times when we wish to put out the fire of anger being directed at us. Most of us have experienced the right use of silence to some degree in this situation. We have walked in assurance of our positions and trusted that truth would prevail.

Most of us, however, probably have not had to consider the use of silence while our lives were being threatened. I want to begin by telling you briefly about a man named Haralan Popov. He exhibited the use of absolute silence with utter peace even in the midst of torture.

Pastor Haralan Popov was a Bulgarian minister. Arrested in 1948 for preaching the Gospel of Christ, he was imprisoned for thirteen years by the Communist regime in "Little Russia," the name then given to Bulgaria. He was beaten, mocked, starved and isolated because of his prominence as a spiritual leader throughout the land. His refusal to renounce his beliefs and forsake the name of Christ led to years of suffering. Though he spoke often of Christ and saw many prisoners converted to Christianity due to his bold speech, there were times he chose silence. Upon his release in 1961, Pastor Popov became the "Voice of the Underground Church." Tens of thousands of Bibles were smuggled into Communist countries due to his efforts.

The book that tells his story, entitled *Tortured for His Faith* (Zondervan, 1970), recounts one time in particular that he chose to stand in silence, literally. He was in prison and was being interrogated. Initially, he tried to answer the question put to him, but when he realized that his assailant was only drawing strength from his speaking, Pastor Popov stopped communicating.

> Mr. Inspector continued to ask me the same question from 8 p.m. to midnight as I stood stiffly. Every 5 or 10 minutes the question was repeated: "Do you know the difference between the militia and the police?" I tried to explain I didn't know. When I saw that I was getting nowhere I stopped answering. He screamed, "We'll teach you a lesson! Hold your arms straight up and don't move a muscle!"

After four hours, Haralan Popov was allowed to lower his arms. This was his first night of torture and interrogation. His gift of knowing when to speak and when to be silent helped Pastor Popov survive tremendous opposition and be used immensely by God.

Pastor Popov is only one example among many who know that at times silence is a better weapon against anger than words. This chapter will help you better understand when to choose silence over speaking out in the face of belligerence.

Techniques of Silence for Reducing Anger

We can be very grateful that most of us will never endure the type of suffering Haralan Popov did during his years of imprisonment. However, there are many times that we find ourselves confronting someone's anger and are unsure how to respond. How do we employ silence in these times? Will speaking really not help the situation? Are emotions so strong that no one is listening? Are we speaking only out of frustration or will our insights be helpful? How can we respond when people are upset with us?

Let us look at some general guidelines to use when involved in a heated discussion. Silence, as in this example of Pastor Popov, can mean just that: not uttering a word. There will be times that the Lord will direct us into that strict measure of self-control. Less obvious, however, is the fact that "silence" can also involve the use of words. Silence does not mean stifling our voices; sometimes, yes, it means not speaking, but it also means choosing our words carefully so that we do not enter into anger ourselves. We silence our rebuttals and defenses and rash comments. Godly silence fosters peace within turmoil. Here are some suggestions:

Do:

1. *Listen.* Be sure to hear what your antagonist is saying. Too often we are so focused on our own thoughts and what

we are going to say that we miss the essence of what the other person is saying.

During my graduate studies, we were asked to role-play counseling sessions with fellow students. These practice sessions were recorded on videotape so we could analyze them later. As we were reviewing one particular session, I saw a glaring weakness in my listening skills. Sue was playing the part of a mother and I was the therapist. I asked Sue to tell me a little about herself. She proceeded to do so.

When she finished, I asked another question: "Do you have any children?" When I saw this on the video, I was shocked and embarrassed. Moments before, when Sue was sharing about herself, she had stated, "I have two children, both girls." I was so busy thinking about what I was going to say next that I did not even hear what she had said. This is a common problem, especially in emotional discussions.

When we ask someone to share information are we listening to the reply? If a person is sharing something we have no interest in, do we tune her out? If someone is upset with us, has a complaint or suggestion, are we willing to hear it?

2. *Clarify.* Ask the person to clarify any areas that are unclear. Do not make assumptions about his intentions. If necessary, ask for an example. When emotionally involved, we often overreact or jump to conclusions.

One morning I left a note for my son Luke to give me a call at my office. Another son, Jason, saw the note and asked what Luke did wrong. I told him that nothing was wrong, that I wanted to ask Luke a question. I found it interesting how often our minds go to the negative—something is wrong, someone is in trouble. This also occurs in discussions when someone feels defensive. We can feel attacked or accused when in reality there is no attack or accusation involved.

3. *Exhaust the list of complaints or concerns.* Once the person has shared his concern(s), ask if there are other issues. Do not begin to defend yourself at this point. It will lead to a type of

tennis match discussion—back and forth—each side vying for points. Allow the person to share all that is on his heart.

This type of "silence" encourages the other person to share his feelings without having to attack you. When taking this approach, you feel in control of your emotions, taking comfort in your chosen response. The alternative, to defend yourself after every issue, usually leads to increased frustration in both participants.

4. Ask for suggestions. Allow the person to give as much input as possible about solutions to the problems presented. It is an interesting fact that if you make a suggestion, it will probably be met with resistance. If given the opportunity, however, the other person may make the same suggestion.

Anyone who is sharing a concern has probably already developed a solution or alternate approach. Give her an opportunity to share what she is thinking. Oftentimes, the suggestions will be workable and helpful. Be willing to hear other ideas—even from those with whom you may be aggravated. Your response should be one of support and appreciation instead of defensiveness. "Where there is no counsel, the people fall" (Proverbs 11:14).

The above suggestions require that we minimize speaking and increase our listening skills. Silence can bring a tremendous sense of peace and empowerment into a life. When I am able to defer to others, allowing them to talk because I have chosen to stay quiet, I gain a sense of confidence regarding my internal control. I feel peace in letting myself be led by the Holy Spirit.

Here, now, are some important things *not* to do when you are the object of anger or misjudgment.

Don't:

1. Don't become self-protective. This is probably the most difficult step, as we do not like anyone to speak negatively about us. This is especially true when we feel misunderstood or there is an incorrect perception.

The phrase "bite your tongue" is a good one to remember when you want to defend yourself. Do not set about to prove your point or convince the other person that he is wrong about you. If his mind is made up or he is not open to your suggestions, your protests will not help. Choosing the techniques of silence given above will make the discussion less painful and it will likely end sooner. "He who is slow to anger is better than the mighty" (Proverbs 16:32).

2. *Don't own problems that belong to others.* Some people have an agenda and will push it at you until they have you hooked into an argument or debate. If you sense that the other person has this in mind, minimize the amount of feedback you give.

Last month Tim came to me and stated that he was not happy that I had not returned his phone call. I told him that I had tried several times, but the line was busy and then no one was home. His response was indicative of his mindset: "When did you call? I was home every night this week. I would have answered the phone." It was obvious he was challenging the validity of my statement and was ready to attack. At that point, I had a couple of choices.

I could choose to think of the night I had called and try to convince Tim of it (which would have been fruitless) or I could take the "silent" approach. I chose the latter. Without being defensive I encouraged him to speak: "Sorry we didn't connect, Tim. I guess we just missed each other. What was it that you wanted to speak to me about?" This started our dialogue and I was able to use some of the strategies that increase sharing.

3. *Don't argue.* As mentioned earlier, a debate will only lead to further frustration. People who are emotionally charged are looking for a fight. Do not let them see you as a target. Use other methods (as described previously) to de-escalate the situation and refrain from arguing.

In a power struggle, no one wins. Each person tries to convince the other and both usually start to feel like volcanoes about to erupt. Anger spews out, feelings get hurt and it becomes harder and harder to sort through the words that were intentional and those thrown into the mix in anger. Apologies and retractions may follow, but the wounds still remain. It is better to be silent than to regret idle words. Allow God to guide your lips and keep you from speaking negatively. "A soft answer turns away wrath, but a harsh word stirs up anger" (Proverbs 15:1).

Avoiding the Anger Trap

There are many ways to take an appropriate escape route when feeling the pressure from the emotion of anger. Bad habits can be eliminated and new healthy patterns can be learned. Instead of seeking revenge, becoming bitter or allowing anger to distort your life perspective, consider utilizing the following suggestions to avoid the anger trap.

1. *Forgive those who have hurt you.* Step back and look at the situation. You may want to communicate your feelings with the other person, but do so in a manner that will not hurt or create defensiveness in him. Follow the principles that we discussed earlier about speaking up. "Therefore, as the elect of God, holy and beloved, put on tender mercies, kindness, humbleness of mind, meekness, longsuffering; bearing with one another, and forgiving one another, if anyone has a complaint against another; even as Christ forgave you, so you also must do" (Colossians 3:12–13).

I recently talked with Andy, an individual who was seething with anger. He refused to attend church or to communicate with friends and he spoke words of hatred toward two specific people. His rationale for such behavior was astounding. Five years ago, he was emotionally wounded by this couple's actions. Though those individuals have asked for his forgiveness, he has refused to release them from his hostility. Those former friends recently moved into town and are attending the same church as Andy; therefore, Andy has left the church. He also expressed anger at his pastor for allowing the couple to come to church in light of their past "sins." Andy will turn from a bitter young man into a bitter old man unless he allows the forgiveness of God to infiltrate his life.

2. *Don't justify your anger.* Getting angry is not wrong. We can be angry and not sin. But when we try to rationalize our angry behavior or excuse our actions through comments like "They deserved it" or "It was their fault," we mask our own responsibility in the situation. We can choose how to respond with our anger. Do we seek revenge, attack, strike back by attempting to injure the person emotionally or physically? Do we withdraw, refusing to engage in meaningful conversation? With our children, do we speak harsh, critical words that wound them? Again, our anger is not the issue. The important issue is whether or not we allow our anger to control our responses. "'Be angry, and do not sin': do not let the sun go down on your wrath" (Ephesians 4:26).

When I was working in the school system as a social worker, I ran into many incidents of parents losing control of their emotions and letting anger rule them. During one such encounter, a father attempted to justify slapping his seven-year-old daughter repeatedly across her face. "I was raised that kids don't smart off to their father," he said. "If I got out of line, I was hit and I turned out okay. I was raised that way and my kids will be, too." We had a strong discussion on the issues of child abuse as well as precautionary measures that would be taken by the school and legal authorities.

3. *Express your needs.* Be willing to verbalize what you are feeling. If you need time alone, tell those around you. If it would be easier to talk at another time or with(out) certain people, share that with others. It is imperative not to stifle or "stuff" your emotions during this time. Once you express your

needs, others will be able to connect with you and to build a bridge of emotions toward you, and vice versa.

During the initial years of our marriage, Joyce and I had an interaction that shaped the way we handled future differences between us. The conflict was not monumental but the emotional separation between us was significant. At one point in my exasperation I said, "Joyce, what do you want from me?" Her response was enlightening: "I feel so far from you. It scares me. I just need you to hold me." As I held her, the anger and frustration melted and we were able to discuss the issues.

Now when a disagreement occurs we sit down, hold hands and talk. We are careful to speak affirming words of love and commitment to one another. "I know we don't agree, but I do love you and we can work this out. From my perspective, here is what I need. . . ." While you may not be able to use this exact process with your boss or friends (they may not appreciate the hug), you can still speak words of support during this time. "I understand we don't agree about this issue, but I am a committed employee and want to resolve this with you. This is what would help me. . . ."

4. *Be accountable to others with your emotions.* Do you allow others to help you stay calm? When you begin to rise up in anger can anyone help you become redirected? Like Naaman and his response to his servants, would you allow others to speak to you when anger begins to control you? We often respond in defensiveness if someone points out a character flaw or area of deficiency in our lives. Be open to others encouraging and guiding you.

When my oldest son, Jason, was a teenager he shared with me that he felt I was "always" getting angry with him. While I did not agree, I realized his perception was important. I told Jason that whenever he felt I was getting angry, he should point it out to me. I gave him permission to stop whatever was occurring and to say, "Dad, this is one of those times I feel you are getting angry." And there were some times he shared this with me. I was able to stop, refocus and start again with my son. This also helped Jason see that there were not as many incidences as he had once thought. While it was awkward for me to receive my son's correction, especially when I felt frustrated with his actions, I did not want to develop a pattern of angry responses with my child.

5. *Take care of yourself.* We must be cautious not to wear ourselves out in life. Taking care of ourselves is an important factor in handling stress and anger. Do you exercise, eat healthy foods, take time to read, listen to music, go for walks? Are you maintaining a strong spiritual balance in life? Are you attending church, reading the Bible, having daily devotions or prayer times? Have you isolated yourself from your friends? Maintaining fellowship with godly people is an important part of a healthy lifestyle. A friend can often be the one to speak into your life and guide you back onto the path of holiness.

One Final Thought . . .

Our daily interactions and conversations will touch areas of frustration and anger and will ultimately test our sense of peace. We must be wise in knowing the appropriate and effective times to share our emotions and when we are to remain silent. God desires for each of us to bring restoration into our relationships with others. There will be times, however, that restoration or reconciliation is challenged and prevented by the attitudes of others. It is during this time that we each need to seek the wisdom of God and understand the purpose of silence.

1. Can you remember a time when you chose to be silent instead of speaking up?
2. When you feel angry or upset, what steps do you take to ensure you do not allow your anger to control you?

nine

Taking a Stand

A man has joy by the answer of his mouth, and a word spoken in due season, how good it is!

Proverbs 15:23

The principles we have learned about speaking up and remaining silent at appropriate times all start with the ability to make good decisions. Understanding God's purposes for our lives—and making decisions that reflect those purposes—helps us grow in our determination and success at taking a stand for what we believe is right.

And our decisions do not affect only ourselves. You and I might never be CEO of a company, President of the United States or in charge of hundreds of people, but it is reasonable to suggest that each one of us will have the opportunity to make decisions that will affect other people. In our homes, churches, schools, businesses, the decisions we make will affect lives for many years to come.

In this sense we are all leaders, and leadership carries great responsibility. Do you think that you are not a leader? Then think again! Leaders are people just like us who chose to take a stand with their voices or their silence. That is what makes an Abraham or Moses or Deborah or Timothy or Mary—or a Ghandi or George Washington!

I believe that leaders are made, not born; their characters are developed and honed by the decisions they make every day to stand for what is right. While we all may have opportunities for leadership within our own spheres of influence, the way we prepare ourselves for these opportunities is the critical component of success.

When you consider the powerful influences around us to do harm instead of good, you realize how easy it is to fail to take a stand for what is right. How do we avoid falling into confusion from the influence of people like Haman, Korah, Jezebel, Judas or the Pharisees? How do we avoid making poor decisions? After all, words of manipulation or pressure may come from any direction. King David was conned by Ziba into taking away land from Mephibosheth, the son of Jonathan (see 2 Samuel 16). Samson was duped by Delilah (see Judges 16). Diotrephes led church members astray until John wrote a letter of rebuke and clarification (see 3 John). Keith convinced Michael to sneak out of the house at night to get back at a fellow student (see Michael Sedler bio, age twelve). Let me explain this one a little further.

Learning the Hard Way

One fine spring day, my buddy Keith and I prepared to create a mild disturbance in our sixth grade class. Our teacher, Mr. Amps, was unaware of this undercurrent of misbehavior. He was about to find out. The windows of our classroom were open to let in the cool breezes, and under the windows sat several stink bombs ready to be lit.

Here was the plan. Keith brought several small stink bombs to school that day with an idea of how we could disrupt the class. While supposedly in the bathroom, we would light the fuses. Then we would return quickly to the classroom, thereby establishing an alibi. Soon the stench would disrupt our class work. Though it sounded risky, I admitted that it would be fun.

The plan unfolded perfectly. Our room had to be evacuated and we all spent the next hour outside. Naturally, Keith and I acted as surprised as everyone else. But, as with most schemes, there were a few small glitches. Several kids figured out what we had been up to during our "bathroom break." Rose was one of them. With a look of disgust, she threw a few critical remarks our way. "How juvenile! Now we will miss recess to make up for class time. Why don't you guys grow up? I have a mind to tell the teacher on you." While her words bothered me very little, Keith was outraged. Rose did not tell and our teacher never found out who created the pungent odor. However, if you are reading this story, Mr. Amps, remember, it was all Keith's idea.

Later that day, Keith convinced me that Rose needed to be taught a lesson. He suggested we sneak out of our houses at night and go throw eggs at her house. Yes, this sounded fun and quite appropriate for our level of maturity. Still, I knew that my parents would not look kindly at my sneaking out and damaging someone else's property. And what Rose said was not really a big issue to me. I tried to talk Keith out of it and make excuses as to why I could not participate. Really!

At eleven P.M., I found myself meeting Keith on the street in front of Rose's house. The plan was simple. Throw several eggs at the house in general and her bedroom window in particular. Then, run as fast as we could back to our respective houses. We would be in bed before they even knew what had happened.

Unfortunately for us, this plan did not go so smoothly. Before we had thrown more than one or two eggs, her parents drove up. They had gone to a movie and were returning home. We were caught red-handed. So stunned by this turn of events, we did not even try to run away. Her parents knew us well and there was no sense in trying to hide. We spent the next weekend washing their house, cleaning their cars and doing yard work.

As I look back over my childhood, I realize that this is not the only time that I was part of a plan that involved stink bombs, eggs, toilet paper or firecrackers. Are these typical childish ventures? Perhaps. My point in sharing this is neither to point out my immature behavior as a young boy nor to illustrate my obvious delinquency characteristics in childhood. That would take too many pages of this book.

Instead, I want to focus on the way in which I was so easily led (or followed) into areas of difficulty. I knew better. My parents were strong in their morals and values and taught each one of their children right from wrong. Yet it took me many years to be able to say no in areas that I did not want to participate in. What created this pattern of complicity instead of standing up for what I knew was proper?

- Was it insecurity and a need for acceptance?
- Was it a desire to be part of a group?
- Was it anger toward others?
- Was it rebellion against my parents or the establishment (as we called it in the 1960s)?
- Was it a sense of revenge against people in general?
- Was it a desire for excitement and the thrill of danger?
- Was it a fear of rejection?

It may have been any one of these or a combination. Regardless, as I grew older I knew that I needed to find a way to take a stand and grow more mature in my decision-making and my leadership potential. It was not until I became a Christian that I chose to make clearer distinctions between right and wrong.

So how do we avoid getting caught up in making poor decisions based on negative input from people around us? No one is immune from making mistakes. Over the years, I have developed decision-making criteria for myself that have greatly aided me in my desire to be a leader and not fall prey to peer pressure and poor individual choices. While I am not guaranteed a flawless decision-making process, the following three guidelines help me minimize my personal mistakes.

1. *I have surrounded myself with people who have a strong relationship with God.* It is critical to have friends who have godly values and a strong sense of conscience. This is what helped King David—he was surrounded by his mighty men. The disciples gave strength to one another and to Jesus (most of the time). And the apostle Paul's letters affirm over and over the solid relationships he had with friends. If the people around us do not have a healthy moral foundation, we will be more likely to ignore our own internal moral compass. The more support systems and areas of accountability that surround us, the more checks and balances we have to help us.

2. *I know these people are faithful to speak the truth.* As we have discussed in this book, there are times we know right from wrong yet do not speak up. While having solid moral people around me is important, unless they are willing to talk about their lives, their faith and belief systems, I may never know their true feelings. I want friends and colleagues who speak out on issues of life without fear of reprisal.

3. *I know these people are bold enough to speak the truth to me.* This area is probably the most important. Unless these friends are willing to confront me, they are not fulfilling their duty as friends. We all need people who love us so much

they will speak honestly and truthfully to us, regardless of our responses.

Following these guidelines has saved me from making life-altering mistakes. I value my friends and their honesty with me.

A strong leader knows when to follow good advice and when to resist manipulation. Noah refused to be swayed by those who mocked and ridiculed him for building an ark. Daniel did not bend to the pressure regarding eating the king's food. Jesus withstood the threats and attacks of the chief priests.

You and I, too, at times have stared manipulation in the face and taken a stand for good. Sometimes we even sense that we might change the mind of the opposition if only we knew how. This brings us to another question in our quest for learning to take a stand: Is it possible to make an appeal to those who oppose us? Yes, I believe it is, and our best examples come from Scripture. God teaches us that He Himself can be appealed to; the principles He shows us help us approach our fellow men as well.

Making a Godly Appeal

Let's start with a man who has already taught us much about speech and silence through his experiences: Abraham. In the book of Genesis we read that God was about to destroy the cities of Sodom and Gomorrah because of their wickedness and depravity. God told Abraham His plan and the Bible says that "Abraham . . . stood before the LORD" (Genesis 18:22). Then out of concern for the righteous people who might live in the cities, Abraham made an appeal to God for their lives. He did not beg, whine or complain. He followed a godly process as he beseeched God to reconsider His plan.

First, Abraham asked God to spare the cities of Sodom and Gomorrah if fifty righteous people could be found in them. To this, God assented. Abraham approached God again and asked if He would spare the cities if forty-five were found. Again, God agreed. Sensing the compassion within the Father, Abraham again sought for mercy if forty righteous people were found. To this, God also agreed. This appeal process continued as Abraham asked about thirty people, then twenty. Finally, Abraham approached God with one final question.

> And he said, "Let not the Lord be angry, and I will speak but once more: Suppose ten should be found there?" And He said, "I will not destroy it for the sake of ten."
>
> Genesis 18:32

It is sad to note that not even ten were found and the cities were burned to ash, but Abraham learned about the importance of making appeals.

Moses also found that he could appeal to God. After Moses returned with the Ten Commandments and found the people worshiping idols and the golden calf, God was ready to destroy the Israelites.

> Then Moses pleaded with the LORD his God, and said: "LORD, why does Your wrath burn hot against Your people whom You have brought out of the land of Egypt with great power and with a mighty hand? Why should the Egyptians speak, and say, 'He brought them out to harm them, to kill them in the mountains, and to consume them from the face of the earth'?" . . . So the LORD relented from the harm which He said He would do to His people.
>
> Exodus 32:11–12, 14

The Lord also taught King Hezekiah about making appeals. Hezekiah was sick and near death. The Lord told him to get his affairs in order as his days were numbered. But Hezekiah made an appeal to God. "'Remember now, O LORD, I pray, how I have walked before You in truth and with a loyal heart, and have done what was good in Your sight.' And Hezekiah wept bitterly" (2 Kings 20:3).

God responded to this appeal of Hezekiah: "I have heard your prayer, I have seen your tears; surely I will heal you" (2 Kings 20:5).

Though God relented and allowed Hezekiah to live several more years, it led to an unpleasant end to King Hezekiah's previously successful reign. In his remaining years, he fell into idol worship, led the nation astray and fathered Manassah, perhaps the most wicked king in Israel's history. When making appeals, be sure your motivation is pure and within the purposes of the will of God.

Now, God is a compassionate teacher and desires the good of His people. Our fellow man is not generally so gracious; our appeals may or may not get affirmative responses. When Jonathan appealed to his father, King Saul, to stop pursuing David, Saul's response was one of the more extreme negative answers: "And Jonathan answered Saul his father, and said to him, 'Why should he [David] be killed? What has he done?' Then Saul cast a spear at [Jonathan] to kill him, by which Jonathan knew that it was determined by his father to kill David" (1 Samuel 20:32–33).

No, not all appeals that we make in accordance with our decision-making will go as planned. Here are a few suggestions to increase the likelihood of success.

1. Be sure to show honor and respect for the person to whom you make your appeal. Both Abraham and Moses affirmed God's position of supremacy and even used it as a basis for their pleas. "Far be it from You!" said Abraham. "Shall not the Judge of all the earth do right?" And Moses reminded God of His great power and mighty hand in bringing the Israelites out of Egypt. Would God now set Himself up for ridicule by destroying His own people?

116

2. Be sure to show an attitude of humility and helpfulness. Be willing to be flexible and compromise. Do not be rigid in your appeal. These three men make suggestions, not demands.

3. Let your goal be a desire to see the will of God break forth. Abraham, Moses and Hezekiah were loyal to God throughout their lives and wanted to be a blessing to others. Our desire should be to help others, not to benefit ourselves.

4. Regardless of the outcome, be willing to support the final decision—assuming, of course, that it does not require you to violate your faith. Each of these men showed willingness to trust in God's ruling.

Suppose, however, that you are asked to do something that violates your own belief system or morality. If the person asking is your supervisor or one in authority, do you need to submit? Are you able to make an appeal? And what if the answer is no? This area is indeed difficult and uncomfortable, but I see a biblical process to follow. Be aware that it is not without potential consequences.

Approach the person and let him know of your conflict. For example, "You have asked me to write down total receipts of two hundred dollars, but we actually made three hundred dollars. I am uncomfortable with doing this and feel it necessary to report the accurate amount." Notice that you do not say, "You are lying, cheating or being dishonest." Remember the areas of successful and effective communication that we have discussed in this book. Avoid putting the person on the defensive and attacking his character.

If the individual responds in an affirming way, you may "have gained your brother" (Matthew 18:15). If the individual, as your supervisor, insists that you follow his directions, go to plan B: "I understand you want me to do this, but again, I feel obligated to be accurate in my report. I enjoy working here and would like to continue to be a part of this company, but I must be able to follow my own moral conscience. I hope

117

you respect this and understand my desire to be a person of honesty and integrity."

You will have to trust God with the results. You may find that you receive new respect and admiration from the supervisor, or you may find yourself spending the next day looking through the want ads for another job. Either way, you will be able to look yourself in the mirror and feel a sense of honor. I want to be able to stand before my God and hear His voice saying, "Well done, good and faithful servant."

5. *Remember that an appeal is a request for help.* It is not intended to engage another in adversarial dealings. It is a straightforward plea for consideration or reconsideration. We should approach the other person in respect and honor, being willing to hear an answer contrary to our will—"submitting to one another in the fear of God" (Ephesians 5:21).

Here are two examples. Make an appeal if someone asks you to do something that conflicts with your preferences. For example, if I ask my son to clean his room but he wants to watch television, he may make an appeal. And make an appeal if you are asked to do something one way but you see a more effective solution. Perhaps you have been asked to complete a project a specific way, but you see another way of finishing it in less time and with greater accuracy.

6. *Make sure that you have a right relationship with God prior to making an appeal.* The point of an appeal is not to manipulate a person or situation. It should not be made for selfish reasons at the cost of another person's reputation, character or benefit. This is why it is so vital for us to be pure and clean in God's sight. This is what allowed the prophets of old to make successful appeals to God.

As long as we are in a right relationship with God, we increase the likelihood that our appeals will be heard. We may make appeals regarding mistakes, errors, differing perspectives or preferences. Others will likely sense the basis for decisions that have been made with pure motives and be more open to us.

How do I know if my spirit is pure or my attitude is right? I ask myself the following questions:

- Is my real concern to further my own agenda, to gain favor in the sight of others or to protect my reputation?
- When I make the appeal, will those I am approaching agree that I am doing so with an attitude of gratefulness, support and encouragement?
- Have I prayed about this appeal? Have I taken counsel with others?
- Will I graciously receive an answer contrary to my will?
- Have I examined the possibility that I may be wrong?

7. *Choose your words carefully.* Use words that will not inflame the situation and create disunity. Give a clear presentation of the facts and your perspective. Avoid embellishing or attacking. Remember that you are sharing from your own personal viewpoint and may not understand the larger picture.

8. *And, finally, if your appeal is turned down, do not lose heart.* The way you approached the person may win him over ultimately. He may decide to listen to you and change his mind. This is exactly what happened to a woman from Canaan who approached Jesus.

And behold, a woman of Canaan came from that region and cried out to Him, saying, "Have mercy on me, O Lord, Son of David! My daughter is severely demon-possessed." But He answered her not a word. And His disciples came and urged Him, saying, "Send her away, for she cries out after us." But He answered and said, "'I was not sent except to the lost sheep of the house of Israel." Then she came and worshiped Him, saying, "Lord, help me!" But He answered and said, "It is not good to take the children's bread and throw it to the little dogs." And she said, "True, Lord, yet even the little dogs eat the crumbs which fall from their master's table." Then Jesus answered and said to her, "O woman, great is your faith! Let it be to you as you desire." And her daughter was healed from that very hour.

Matthew 15:22–28

A right response, even if the appeal has been rejected, may bring us into favor with those we are approaching.

To choose the right words, to present ourselves with the appropriate demeanor, to take the time to connect with another person—each of these will affect the outcome of the decisions we make to resist manipulation and stand for our beliefs. And even if our appeals are rejected, we may find ourselves growing in favor with those we have approached.

One Final Thought . . .

Before approaching an individual regarding a problem or area of frustration, take the time to pray and be sure you have a right spirit. If you do not have time to pray, you do not have time to communicate with others.

1. Think of a time when you made a decision and stood behind it. What did you learn from the outcome?
2. What pitfalls or traps seem to get in the way of your decision-making? Do you feel that there is any value in making appeals? Why or why not? What does this say about your confidence in your decisions?

ten

Winning the Race

The Pessimist sees difficulty in every opportunity. The Optimist sees opportunity in every difficulty.

Winston Churchill

History is sprinkled with stories of people who chose godly silence as well as those who spoke up with a godly voice. Countries were spared the destruction of war and the devastation of death due to their discernment and boldness. Whether refusing to speak or refusing to be silent, these individuals let God guide them regardless of the consequences.

As you read this chapter, it is my hope that a surge of inspiration will flood your life. You may choose to read and reread this chapter for encouragement. The people I have chosen to honor here are only a miniscule sampling of heroes throughout history. Each and every day, new heroes are emerging and laying a firm foundation of faith and strength for generations to come. Will you be one of those new voices? Certainly, many heroes in the upcoming pages might have said, "No, not me," yet here they are. Perhaps a more important question for each of us is: "Am I willing to be a voice, a destiny-maker in life?" To that let us all say, "Yes, and amen!" May the testimonies found in the following pages inspire each one of us to greatness and to be a voice of action.

Dr. Martin Luther King, Jr., often spoke about the importance of one's voice. He challenged each person to find the strength within to stand up to prejudice and ungodly actions. At times, he considered silence to be a form of self-preservation. He had witnessed how words could distort the truth and manipulate the environment. Our voices must be used for clarity and truth, not for deception and deceit. In the following speech taken from his book *Strength to Love* (Augsburg, 1986), Dr. King challenged each one of us to reassess our tendency to use our voices for our own benefit, to attempt to convince others we are right even when clearly wrong.

> Midnight is the hour when men desperately seek to obey the eleventh commandment, "Thou shalt not get caught." According to the ethic of midnight, the cardinal sin is to be caught and the cardinal virtue is to get by. It is all right to lie, but one must lie with real finesse. It is all right to steal, if one is so dignified that, if caught, the charge becomes embezzlement, not robbery. It is permissible even to hate, if one so dresses his hating in the garments of love that hating appears to be loving. The Darwinian concept of the survival of the fittest has been substituted by a philosophy of the survival of the slickest. This mentality has brought a tragic breakdown of moral standards, and the midnight of moral degeneration deepens.

I have noticed that some of my "speaking out in action" is simply a cover-up for my own mistakes and errors. I try to justify my position and my attitudes. A careful use of words can mean a clever distortion of truth, and the situation shifts in my favor.

Some time ago, my wife asked if I would clean out our garage and straighten up the pile of tools, wood, paint cans and other collectibles. My answer of affirmation was met with a warm smile and hug. Weeks went by, but the garage remained unchanged. One day I noticed Joyce eyeing the garage with frustration. She knew that the following weekends were filled with activities, none that included the garage. Being an astute observer of nonverbal communication (I will wait until the laughter subsides), I knew I had to act quickly.

Later that day, I announced boldly that I was dedicating the upcoming Saturday to cleaning the garage. I mentioned pointedly how busy I had been with work and doing other chores around the house, but I knew the garage was important to her. I bemoaned the fact that, due to my hectic schedule, I was unable to complete the cleaning earlier in the spring. My wife, also an astute observer, read my motivation. She smiled lovingly and said, "Oh, too bad you won't be able to join us on Saturday when the boys and I go golfing. If only you had done the garage earlier in the month, we could have all gone golfing together." The dagger of truth went deep.

Yes, as Dr. King stated, I move often into an area he called "survival of the slickest." Am I alone or will some of you hold up the mirror of self-confrontation and join me? You see, although I may be able to shade the appearance of truth, even convince others that I am right, in reality I have only prospered by misguided perceptions, selfish thoughts, dishonesty and actions of deceit.

So, we can see that maintaining integrity means much more than mere words. Our motives, attitudes and purposes for speaking out have a significant impact on the purity of our messages. What are my motives? Do I take a stand in stubbornness? Am I open to hearing other opinions and willing to be challenged without getting defensive? I have to ask myself these questions regularly.

Receiving Guidance

Several years ago, a situation made such an impression on me that it has forever changed the way I respond to guidance and correction. I had spent many hours counseling and working with Ryan, who attended our church. His reluctance and hesitancy to change and modify some of his behaviors had created unnecessary pain and chaos in many lives. Ryan insisted on degrading certain people and twisting specific events so as to benefit himself. His distortions and lies caused major problems in the church and community. The leaders of our church agreed that we should not confront Ryan one-on-one; we decided to have at least one other person present when talking with him in order to avoid further problems. His pattern of remembering events inaccurately had put more than one person in an awkward position.

One day as I was praying, I sensed a certain direction that I could take with Ryan. I felt sure that it would facilitate a change in him. I went immediately to his place of business and met with him for over two hours. Although the process was laborious, I held fast to my plan and spoke words of honesty, truth and direction. By the completion of our meeting, I felt that tremendous clarity had been accomplished in his life. We hugged one another and I saw a new sense of freedom appear on his face.

The next day I sat with the leadership of our church and began to share about the fantastic meeting I had had with Ryan. As I shared, the looks of confusion and dismay on the faces of my friends caused defensiveness to rise up within me. Once I stopped talking, the questions began to come at a rapid-fire pace.

"Did you go by yourself?" one leader asked.

"Didn't we all agree last week not to counsel Ryan alone?" another one said.

And finally, "Mike, I don't understand. It seems that you totally disregarded the agreement we all came to in a recent meeting. Is that true?"

I stated that I did remember that meeting, but surely the inspiration I had as well as the excellent meeting with Ryan should cover any overzealousness on my part. They did not agree.

My defensiveness led to a few tense moments. After twenty minutes of excuses on my part, I looked around the table. I saw people who cared about me, who wanted success for me, but who also disagreed with me. As my spirit softened, I knew what needed to occur. I asked my colleagues for forgiveness. "I am not sure what I did wrong," I said. " But if all of you feel that I was incorrect in my action, I need to ask your forgiveness and try to get a clearer understanding." I left the meeting discouraged and upset.

When I arrived home, Joyce asked how my day went. My reply was terse with a bit of tongue-in-cheek: "Just splendid. We had 'roast Mike' for lunch." While Joyce commiserated with my pain, she did not feed my self-pity (much to my chagrin). Over the next several days, we prayed and discussed the situation. I came to realize that my independent nature had encouraged me to act rashly and to minimize, even discard, the guidance and wisdom of my fellow leaders. In a candid discussion with my wife, she shared how that same attitude from me creeps into our marriage and shuts her off from my life. With a heart of gratefulness, I asked Joyce for forgiveness and thanked her for her honesty.

In the upcoming days, I went to each member of the leadership team and again asked for forgiveness. Only this time, I felt a deeper understanding of my own arrogance and pride. I then asked each of them (as I did my wife) to challenge me, guide me and correct me if they ever saw this pattern in my life again. Interestingly, within a week or two I heard from some other friends that Ryan was bad-mouthing people, including me, for our attitudes toward him. My inspiration for Ryan had failed to inspire change in him. However, it had a powerful impact on me.

Because of that experience, I have established some firm guidelines in my life when receiving guidance or correction.

Do:

1. Listen to what your friends and colleagues are saying, especially if it is contrary to your perspective. (Remember in chapter 3 the example of Naaman receiving guidance from his servants?) That others see the same issue differently may be significant and broaden your viewpoint.
2. Ask for examples or specifics to help you understand. It does not take too many examples to help us see a clearer picture. Be careful. Our tendency is to discount others' examples as "exceptions rather than the rule."
3. Recognize that you may be wrong. Yes, this is possible. The mere fact that other people are pointing out a contrary position should alert you to the fact that there may be more than one side to the issue.
4. Repent and ask forgiveness if you sense that others feel violated. Whether I intended to inflict pain or not—be it emotional, mental or physical—if a person has been damaged, it is appropriate to ask for forgiveness.
5. Thank the person for the honesty and willingness to share his or her perspective. To share an opposing viewpoint risks retaliation. Appreciate the faithfulness of your friends to speak the truth in love.
6. Set up a follow-up time to share your insights and obtain further feedback as part of the accountability process.

Don't:

1. Don't be pre-judge. Listen attentively to what is being said and avoid making excuses. Our tendency is to discount the examples and to excuse away the feelings of others. Granted, the "other person" may not understand. However, it is possible you are "the other person."
2. Don't attack others with phrases like, "You just don't understand." Words of defensiveness only create a barrier to further communication. If they do not understand, find ways to communicate understanding, not separation.
3. Don't argue by stating your position over and over. If someone does not agree the first time, the next five times will not convince them. Saying it louder and with greater force will not work either.
4. Don't keep playing the "tapes" of the conversation over and over in your head. Conversations and events will get distorted and you will begin to become offended by your new interpretation.

Our tendency is to become defensive when others disagree with us. Remember, these are people who care about us. They share their opinions because they love us and want us to grow personally or professionally. We must be willing to hear their concerns and we must be open to change.

We talked about motives in an earlier chapter, but this is a good "checkpoint." If our motives are pure, we:

- will not feel a need to argue and fight with people about our beliefs, opinions or actions.
- will desire to help others understand our perspective without alienating them.
- will be satisfied to share confidently, believing that "truth" will be understood in time.

- will not assault others verbally, making comments about their character, attitude or choices in life.
- will be open to discussions and understand that people might need time to process our words.
- will not respond with anger toward those who disagree with us. Instead, we will try to garner their trust and find a more opportune time during which to share our point of view.

What about those whose motives are not pure—bullies whose tactics may include berating others, yelling, screaming? It is not uncommon for bullies to attack a person's age, color, religion, intelligence, maturity or culture. Those with impure motives attempt to intimidate others into a particular course of action. People with impure motives may use hatred as a weapon to create dissension and disunity. They may use pressure tactics or prey upon one's fear or insecurity. They may make threats in order to manipulate others' emotions.

There will always be those whose voices are used to pollute, to contaminate and to injure others. Their voices are so strong, so forceful that their victims can become paralyzed in silence. They sound so convincing, so sure of themselves, they seem to be right at the time.

It is easy for our confidence to dwindle in the face of bullying rhetoric. Confusion and paralysis fall upon us while words of poison infiltrate among the people. We must be careful. We must be wise. We must be willing to be a voice of action in the midst of confusion. If we are not cautious, our very voices may be silenced by intimidation. This quote by Gerhard Weinberg, which I read on the Encarta Online Encyclopedia, reminds us how silence allowed one man to infect an entire nation.

In 1933, Adolf Hitler initiated policies to rid the Aryan race of undesirable elements and eliminate other races that he considered inferior and dangerous to the Germans. First, the government approved marriage loans to the "right kind" of Germans—those whose ancestors and appearance measured up to the Nazi's standard of Aryan purity. These loans were repaid as the newlyweds produced babies. To discourage the propagation of the "wrong kind" of people, a law required compulsory sterilization of men and women deemed likely to have defective babies, primarily those with physical and mental handicaps. By 1945 some 400,000 Germans had been sterilized.

Hitler was a voice, a powerful voice, of intimidation and contamination. How many ungodly voices have resulted in screams of agony, torment and misery? The history books (and current newspapers) are full of voices like Pharaoh, Herod, Stalin, Amin, Khomeini, bin Laden . . . voices that have caused suffering and death for millions. Weinberg continues:

> The first discriminatory laws against the Jews also came in 1933. These laws barred Jews from government employment and restricted their admission to universities. In subsequent years, the anti-Semitic laws became increasingly harsh, as Jews were deprived of citizenship, excluded from more and more jobs, forbidden to own cars, thrown out of public schools, and stripped of property. These events culminated in "Kristallnacht" (the "Night of Broken Glass"), the night of November 9, 1938, when Nazi mobs killed dozens of Jews, smashed thousands of windows in Jewish neighborhoods, and set fire to almost all Jewish houses of worship throughout Germany. Following Kristallnacht, the Nazis sent more than 30,000 Jews to concentration camps. Hundreds of thousands of others fled the country.

Who Will Take a Stand?

A voice may be strong; it may be loud; and it may be convincing. That does not mean it should be followed. Where were the voices of honor as the Nazi army infiltrated Austria?

How many people shrugged and said, "It's not my country." From Czechoslovakia and Hungary came the whispers, "If we are silent, maybe they will go away." Soon questions arose in Lithuania and Poland: "Is it too late to speak?" Hatred, separation, lies and fear had contaminated the surrounding countries of Eastern Europe. Silence had spoken loudly, resoundingly—and its destruction was devastating.

Were there any righteous voices? Yes, they were there. They were firm and resolute in their purpose and desire to prevent the destruction of a people. Look at this passage from *The Hiding Place* by Corrie ten Boom:

And the very next morning into the shop walked the perfect solution. He was a clergyman friend of ours, pastor in a small town outside of Haarlem, and his home was set back from the street in a large wooded park.

"Good morning, Pastor," I said, the pieces of the puzzle falling together in my mind. "Can I help you?"

I looked at the watch he had brought in for repair. It required a very hard-to-find spare part. "But for you, Pastor, we will do our very best. And now I have something I want to confess."

The pastor's eyes clouded, "Confess?"

I drew him out the back door of the shop and up the stairs to the dining room.

"I confess that I too am searching for something." The pastor's face was now wrinkled with a frown. "Would you be willing to take a Jewish mother and her baby into your home? They will almost certainly be arrested otherwise."

Color drained from the man's face. He took a step back from me. "Miss ten Boom! I hope you're not involved with any of this illegal concealment and undercover business. It's just not safe! Think of your father! And your sister—she's never been strong!"

On impulse I told the pastor to wait and ran upstairs. Betsie had put the newcomers in Willem's old room, the farthest from windows on the street. I asked the mother's permission to borrow the infant: the little thing weighed hardly anything in my arms.

Back in the dining room I pulled back the coverlet from the baby's face.

There was a long silence. The man bent forward, his hand in spite of himself reaching for the tiny fist curled round the blanket. For a moment I saw compassion and fear struggle in his face. Then he straightened. "No. Definitely not. We could lose our lives for that Jewish child!"

Unseen by either of us, Father had appeared in the doorway. "Give the child to me, Corrie," he said.

Father held the baby close, his white beard brushing its cheek, looking into the little face with eyes as blue and innocent as the baby's own. At last he looked up at the pastor. "You say we could lose our lives for this child. I would consider that the greatest honor that could come to my family."

The pastor turned sharply on his heels and walked out of the room.

A voice, just one old man's voice. One person willing to take action against the ways of darkness and evil. What happens when one person takes action? Others follow! Paralysis is broken and others listen to the fresh new voice, one that leads to freedom, healing and strength. Of course, this is not always seasy. It takes a strong personal conviction. It requires a person who is willing to endure ridicule, mockery, isolation and rejection. History recounts stories of people who spoke out against the atrocities of the Nazi regime. Their voices protected millions of people from death. The voices came from people like Oscar Schindler, Dietrich Bonhoeffer, Corrie ten Boom, Martin Niemoller, Winston Churchill and many others. Some spoke up verbally while others were moved to silent action. In either case, lives were changed dramatically.

In his first address to the House of Commons, Prime Minister Churchill, age 63, made a stirring appeal and became a strong voice of action.

"You ask what is our policy? I will say: It is to wage war, by sea, land and air, with all our might and with all the strength God can give us; to wage war against a monstrous tyranny, never surpassed in the dark, lamentable catalogue of human crime. That is our policy. You ask, What is our aim? I can answer in one word: Victory—victory at all costs, victory in spite of all terror, victory, however long and hard the road may be; for without victory, there is no survival."

Years later, when then Prime Minister Clement Atlee was asked what Churchill did to win the war, he replied simply, "Talk about it."

What a poignant statement! *He talked about it.* It was not how clever their military strategy was during the war, the force of their guns, ships, planes or troops. It was not their threats, anger or their superior battle plans that won the war. No! It was that Prime Minister Churchill talked about it and was unwilling to hide in fear and intimidation from Hitler's Nazi regime.

Have you ever been in a situation where the words or threats from someone were so intense they caused you to shrink back and lose your voice of action? I have—many times. Each time, inside, I knew that I should say something. And, each time, when I walked away I felt condemned for my silence. I know I am not alone.

Throughout history, silence has numbed our sensitivity. Many kept silent while slavery infected the United States. Voices kept silent as the Native American people were cheated and swindled out of their land and birthright. Even today, silence resounds as millions of babies are conveniently aborted. Where are the voices?

Speaking out is easy if the stakes are small and there are many around to support us, but what about when the cost of speaking out may cost us our reputation, our jobs, our family, or even our lives? What if the cost is prison? Remember Rosa Parks? She was a black woman who, after a full day of working, decided to take a vacant seat on a bus, behind the ten seats reserved for whites. She was arrested in Montgomery, Alabama, in 1955 for refusing to give up her seat to a white man. Her action sparked a national crisis that helped initiate the beginning of reform throughout the country. It was not so much what she said, but what she did. She refused to bow to prejudice and racism. One woman. One voice. One action.

What if the cost for speaking out is death? Will we still be strong in our convictions? Honestly, it is difficult to say. Sure, in the confines of our homes, while reading this book (or writing it as I am today), in boldness and confidence we might say, "Yes, I would die for a cause I believe in," but would we?

What of those who did take a stand, then were tortured and eventually killed? I think of Dietrich Bonhoeffer who, as a Christian minister, spoke forcefully against Hitler and his hatred of the Jewish people. Imprisoned and tortured, he had opportunities to escape, but chose to stay behind to minister to others and to minimize the reprisal against his family. In April 1945, Bonhoeffer was hanged at the extermination camp of Flossenburg. The camp doctor who witnessed the execution wrote:

> I was most deeply moved by the way this lovable man prayed, so devout and so certain that God heard his prayer. At the place of execution, he again said a short prayer and then climbed the steps to the gallows, brave and composed. . . . In the almost fifty years that I worked as a doctor, I have hardly ever seen a man die so entirely submissive to the will of God.

In Foxe's *Christian Martyrs of the World,* we read of heroes who chose death rather than being silent, rather than recanting their beliefs, and rather than running for their lives. One such person was Polycarp, Bishop of Smyrna. After his arrest at the age of 86, he was taken before the tribunal for sentencing. Taking pity on him because of his advanced age, they begged him to deny his belief in Jesus Christ so as to spare his life. "Reproach Christ and I will release you," the proconsul demanded. Polycarp replied, "Eighty-six years I have served Him, and He never once wronged me. How can I blaspheme my King, who saved me?" They then tied him to a stake, gathered wood and lit the fire. When he did not die from the flames, a soldier plunged a sword into him.

A voice of action makes a difference in history. It affects people for generations to come. When we feel like retreating, even running for our lives—as did Elijah—we need a voice of encouragement. When we fear repercussion—as did Peter—we need a voice of direction. When our strength is gone—as it was in the nation of Germany—we need a voice of purpose. This voice may come from a friend, a spouse, a pastor, leader or coworker. It may come during our prayer time, even as a still, small voice. We need to look for a source of support during these trying times.

A friend gave the following poem to me. The author is unknown, but the lesson is vital to everyone who has ever needed the courage to speak up or maintain a godly silence.

> "Quit! Give up, you're beaten!" they shout at me and plead.
> "There's just too much against you now, this time you can't succeed."
> And as I started to hang my head in front of failure's face,
> My downward fall is broken by the memory of a race.
>
> And hope refills my weakened will, as I recall that scene,
> And just the thought of that short race rejuvenates my being.
> A children's race. Young boys, young men. I remember well.
> Excitement, sure, but also fear; it wasn't hard to tell.
>
> They all lined up so full of hope. Each thought to win that race.
> Or tie for first, or if not that, at least take second place.
> And fathers watched from off the side, each cheering for his son,

And each boy hoped to show his dad, that he would be the
    one.

(The whistle blew)
To win, to be the hero there, was each young boy's desire.
And one boy in particular, his dad was in the crowd,
Was running near the lead and thought, *My dad will be so
    proud.*

But as he sped down the field across a shallow dip,
The little boy who thought to win, lost his step and slipped,
Trying hard to catch himself, his hands flew out to brace,
And 'mid the laughter of the crowd, he fell flat on his face.

So, down he fell and with him hope. He couldn't win it
    now.
Embarrassed, sad, he only wished to disappear somehow.
But, as he fell his dad stood up and showed his anxious
    face.
Which to the boy so clearly said, *Get up and win the race!*

He quickly rose, no damage done, behind a bit that's all,
And ran with all his mind and might to make up for his fall.
So anxious to restore himself, to catch up and to win
His mind went faster than his legs. He slipped and fell
    again.

He wished that he had quit before with only one disgrace.
I'm hopeless as a runner now, I shouldn't try to race.
But through the laughing crowd he searched and found his
    father's face—
That steady look that said again, *Get up and win the race!*

So up he jumped to try again, ten yards behind the last,
If I'm to gain those yards, he thought, *I've got to run real fast.*
Expending everything he had, he regained eight or ten,
But trying so hard to catch the lead, he slipped and fell
    again.

Defeat! He lay there silently, a tear dropped from his eye.
There's no sense running anymore, three strikes, I'm out, why
     try?
The will to rise had disappeared, all hope had fled away,
So far behind, so error prone, closer all the way.

I've lost, so what's the use? he thought. *I'll live with my dis-*
     grace.
Get up, an echo sounded low, *get up and take your place.*
You weren't meant for failure here; you haven't lost at all.
For winning is no more than this; to rise each time you fall.

So up he rose to win once more, deciding to commit,
He resolved that win or lose, at least he wouldn't quit.
So far behind the others now, the most he'd ever been,
Still he gave it all he had and ran as though to win.
Three times he'd fallen stumbling, three times he rose again.

They cheered the winning runner as he crossed the line,
     first place,
Head high and proud and happy: no falling, no disgrace.
But when the fallen youngster crossed the finishing line, last
     place,
The crowd gave him the greater cheer for finishing the race.

And even though he came in last, with head bowed low,
     not proud,
You would have thought he'd won the race, to listen to the
     crowd.
And to his dad he sadly said, "I didn't do so well."
"To me you won," his father said, "you rose each time you
     fell."

And now when times seem dark and hard and difficult to
     face,
The memory of that little boy helps me to run my race.
For all of life is like that race, with ups and downs and all,
And all you have to do to win is rise each time you fall.

"Quit! Give up, you're beaten!" they still shout in my face,
But another voice within me says, *Get up and win the race!*

One Final Thought . . .

Silence. Speaking up. Both change destinies. When we use these tools inappropriately, we can do great harm. And when we use them as God intended, we can change our world for the better.

Whether using a godly voice or choosing a godly silence, we must step up—and keep on stepping up—until we win the race. There are multiple times during the course of a day when we may feel pressure and intimidation. Our inadequacies may come to the forefront as we engage in a disagreement or difference of opinion. Regardless, we are to uphold our convictions and allow the truth of God to change hearts. And, as we have discussed, the way I communicate, the words I choose and the timing of my sharing will significantly affect the receptiveness of the message.

Choose wisely whether to speak or to remain silent, whether to confront or to support, and whether to agree or disagree. Never forget that we are all called to be change agents in the Kingdom of God.

1. Think of an important value or belief you have. How far would you go to defend this belief system?
2. Choose one person (or cause) that has inspired you. Spend some time meditating on the impact of the decision to speak or to be silent.

Free at Last

I believe that Jesus Christ is the Son of God.

Michael Sedler, 1977

The words formed in my mouth. I stared at my parents, the two most precious people in my life. They were so supportive, so caring. Yet I was about to shatter their lives and knowingly cause them immense pain. Would this destroy our relationship? Would my family continue to be my family or would they "count me as dead"? It was as if time stood still as I prepared to speak the words that would change my life forever. . . .

I come from a close, loving family. I am the third of four boys. Both sets of grandparents came from Russia. My father and mother transplanted our family from Kansas City, Missouri, to Phoenix, Arizona, when I was five years old. No more snow, but lots of sun.

Dad and Mom always spoke about the importance of family loyalty. I could call my brothers names but would fight anyone else who did. We were taught to stand up for our rights and to vocalize our thoughts. Love, honor and respect were part of the Sedler family.

Another part of the family was our devotion to our belief system. I was raised in a Jewish home and we attended the synagogue Temple Beth Israel faithfully. My parents were raised in the more Orthodox ways of Judaism, but the Orthodox synagogue in Phoenix did not meet with their satisfaction so they chose to attend a Reform synagogue. This meant that some of the more stringent religious laws were not observed in our home. For example, as a child my mother was not allowed to ride in a motorized vehicle during the Sabbath time (Friday sundown to Saturday sundown). We also did not follow some of the dietary laws that many Orthodox Jews observe, such as not eating pork and not serving milk with meat at dinner.

My grandfather was a cantor in the synagogue. He performed much of the song service and assisted the rabbi. Many of the Jewish rituals and traditions that my parents enjoyed in their youth were continued in our home—everything from lighting candles on Friday nights to attending Hebrew school weekly to prepare for our Bar Mitzvah ceremonies at the age of thirteen. Judaism was at the center of my life. The majority of my friends were Jewish, as were my parents' friends. We seemed to gravitate toward people of like faith.

Dirty Jew

Aside from missing several days of public school for Jewish holidays now and then, I never really felt separated from others due to my religious beliefs. Then an incident occurred in my elementary school that brought to the forefront the reality that I was different from some of the other kids at school. I was nine or ten years old. Up to that point I had been unaware of any bigotry or prejudice that may have been directed toward me. I had heard of World War II and the atrocities toward the Jewish people, but I had never fully comprehended the actions in Nazi Germany. Six million was just a large number to me; I was not able to translate that into death as it pertained to the Jewish people in Germany.

On this particular day at school we were playing softball. Suddenly we heard a lot of yelling and screaming going on behind one of the dugouts. As I peered in the direction of the shouting, I saw two boys fighting. They were a couple of years older than I, but I knew both of them. One was the school bully, Danny Teller, and the other was Steve Schwartz, the older brother of a friend of mine. Danny was mocking Steve and laughing at him as he pummeled him with his fists. Steve kicked at Danny and landed a few shots on his face. This only seemed to infuriate Danny more and the beating toward Steve continued.

After what seemed like quite a while, but was probably only a minute or so, a teacher came over and broke up the fight. He asked firmly, "What is going on here?" Danny just smiled and shrugged his shoulders. The teacher turned toward a bloody Steve and repeated his question, this time with more force. Steve, with tears and blood coming down his face said, "He called me a dirty Jew."

I was stunned. I am not sure if I was more surprised that Danny would call him that name or that Steve would get into a fight over it. In any event, the incident heightened my awareness regarding the subject of prejudice. From then on I began to notice routine comments in the newspapers, television, radio and within my own school. Comments like "I Jewed him down," "Jew lover," "dirty Jew" or "Jew boy" suddenly seemed commonplace.

My teenage years were initiated with my Bar Mitzvah, a ceremony where a Jewish boy becomes "a man" or a Jewish girl celebrates womanhood. I was responsible for leading the song service, reading from the Torah and giving a short message. For Christians it is similar to leading praise and worship, reading from the Bible and then giving a sermon—all in all, it meant about an hour of leading the congregation. Except for the sermon, everything was spoken in Hebrew.

In high school I continued my Jewish studies each week and went through a time of confirmation at the age of sixteen. I also was part of a Jewish youth organization. We met each week at the Phoenix Jewish Community Center. We had classes with Jewish leaders in the city, had our own weekend sports league and our own social events. While the members of the organization were from several different synagogues in town, we all rallied under the banner of Judaism. It was a combination of a fraternity and church high school group. We elected officers. (I was vice president one year.) We organized citywide dances for Jewish kids and attended statewide retreats and conferences focused on our Jewish heritage.

My time during these teenage years was split between my Jewish involvement and playing high school baseball. I had always loved sports and was now becoming serious about furthering my baseball opportunities. A scholarship to college was an attainable goal for me. I did not discount, by some incredible opportunity, becoming a professional player. My contact with non-Jews increased, but my closest friends continued to be Jewish. When I went out with girls, whether as friends or on dates, they were Jewish. My parents discouraged any type of dating with gentile girls. Although they did not forbid me from going out with non-Jews, they obviously disapproved.

My oldest brother was married in 1969. His wife converted to Judaism, which made things smooth for most of the family. There was one uncle who would not accept her because she was not a "blood Jew," but others of us fell in love with her. My new sister-in-law had a younger sister. She was sixteen, as was I, so we spent some time together. She began to talk to me about Christianity and about a guy named Jesus.

Honestly, I was sixteen, she was cute and I listened to her so we could talk. I had no idea who this Jesus person was, nor did I care. The idea of someone being God was weird to me. She gave me a Bible and encouraged me to read it. So to have something to talk with her about, I began to read the New Testament.

I read Matthew, then Mark and was halfway through the book of Luke when I became frustrated. *How ridiculous!* I thought. *The Bible has the same stories in each section.* And with that, I quit reading it. At least I knew more about Jesus than I had. I knew that besides walking on water, He was crucified by the Romans and the Jews. And most of the Jewish leaders hated Him.

It was during my high school years that the Vietnam War was coming to a head. Throughout my elementary and high school years, the Civil Rights movement had gained in strength. The drug culture was introduced to the nation, as was a new brand of music brought on by the Fab Four, the Beatles. My high school experiences included an introduction to drugs.

I maintained a good academic foundation, excelled in baseball, involved myself in the Jewish community and immersed myself in drugs. While never participating in the use of needles (heroin was popular during those days), I smoked marijuana regularly and took different types of pills (amphetamines, psychedelics). I was busy my senior year with preparing for college, being a "social butterfly," partying constantly, holding the office of senior class president, receiving a baseball scholarship to a university in California and—unexpectedly—experiencing a touch from God.

Touching God

In the fall of 1972, our annual Jewish Community Conference was held at a retreat house outside of the city area. More than two hundred Jewish teenagers joined together for several days of teaching from Jewish leaders, singing spiritual songs, playing games and socializing. It was a great opportunity to meet new people and to hear interesting aspects about our Jewish culture and heritage. I was not prepared, however, for the impact this particular conference would make upon my life.

Rabbi Avi Goldstein from California was our scheduled speaker. Over the next three days I was mesmerized by his stories of Auschwitz, a concentration camp run during World War II. He spoke of a faith and a belief in the miraculous power of God. He spoke about Israel and the fortitude within the Jewish people. In all my years I had never heard someone speak with such force and conviction about God. Something began to stir within me during this time.

When I returned home, the feeling and hunger for more of God had not departed. In the next few days I spoke with a person at our synagogue who oversaw the religion department. Either I was too familiar with that person or else he did not have the same conviction as Rabbi Goldstein, but my visit was unsatisfactory. I sought out a rabbi from another synagogue within our city.

This rabbi was of a more Orthodox persuasion. His discussion centered only on the importance of the Jews staying together, fighting oppression and not losing hope. Though I agreed with him, this also was not what I was hungering for. I asked him some pointed questions about God and his understanding of faith and miracles. I was stunned when the rabbi discounted miracles of God as mere coincidences—stories that have been exaggerated. He gave credit to the "power of positive thinking" for physical healing. I walked out of his office discouraged.

A final connection with Rabbi Goldstein solidified my disappointment. I wrote him. His reply seemed hollow and lacked the conviction and intensity with which he had shared at the retreat. I became confused and frustrated. It appeared that my Jewish faith was wrapped up in hoping Israel would be safe and perpetuating religious practices without an understanding of God.

Over the next few years I listened closely when I went to synagogue and waited to hear something that would stir me again. It did not happen. Most teachings and discussions from the religious leaders centered on the sovereignty of Israel and the protection of the Jewish people. Where was the faith and strength I had seen portrayed in the movie *Fiddler on the Roof*? Could I talk to God personally? Was there a Creator who actually cared about His people? As the years passed, I began to set aside the thought that God had any place in my life.

In fact, I was surprised to find out that many Jewish people had little insight into the Person of God. The more I asked the more I realized that many Jews do not see God as being active in one's life but more as a Creator with a hands-off policy. Prayer is considered the same as having "good thoughts" rather than being a direct line to God. Somewhere during my college years, I shut off the little nagging feeling of being spiritually bankrupt.

A New World

My years of college were filled with many new experiences. My best friend, Jay, told me after the first quarter of college that he was a homosexual. This was not so much a shock as a point of confusion to me. To my knowledge I had known few gay individuals. Through my friendship with Jay I learned more about bias and prejudice, from his perspective.

I expanded my experiences and enjoyed growing in my love for musicals, ballet, drama and jazz. My circle of friends was wide and diverse. We began to frequent art museums and concerts of varying musical formats. And I continued the familiar route of partying with my friends and playing baseball. I enjoyed my newfound college freedom in California. San Diego is a beautiful city with gorgeous beaches. I spent many hours enjoying the sun and sand. While I kept my grades well above average, academics were not high on my priority list. However, I would have received an *A* in suntan 101.

My senior year of college was a whirlwind. I had come to the understanding that while I loved baseball and was a good player, I was not going to be a great player. Any dream of playing professional baseball gradually dissolved. In addition, my involvement with drugs had affected my desire to play. I preferred partying to practicing baseball. It is one area I came to regret. While there are some areas in which one may obtain a second chance, college athletic eligibility is not one of those.

A significant life experience occurred during spring break of my senior year. I had planned on going to law school and eventually moving into the field of politics. I was getting ready to take the entrance exams for law school in the upcoming weeks. While I was becoming disillusioned with the law field and politics due to Watergate, I felt no other interest luring me.

I needed a few more college credits, so during spring break I signed up for a wilderness survival class. We spent five days in Yosemite National Park, including two days living outside in snow caves. It sounded like a fun way to gain some college credits.

I showed up with my $19.99 Kmart boots I had sprayed with Scotch-Guard water repellant. I had a pair of cloth gloves that would be great on a cool night in San Diego and a polyester sleeping bag. Suffice it to say, I had no idea what I was getting myself into and the leaders of the group did not check our equipment closely. Yes, I nearly froze. One night I wondered if I would ever feel my toes again. Waking up to frozen shoes was horrible.

I learned a lot, but most significantly, I had time to think, be alone and ponder my future. The spiritual longing began to surface again in my life. It was during this time I decided to quit using drugs. I also decided not to go to law school. Instead, I wanted to work with people, perhaps as a social worker. I grew excited about my chosen direction in life.

Our family regularly discussed financial and personal success. The Jewish culture emphasizes accomplishments and recognition. It was important for each of the Sedler boys to go to college, find a profession where he would have financial independence, marry a nice Jewish girl and have a wonderful life.

My oldest brother was a captain in the Marines, received a master's degree in business and has worked for some of the leading tax and technology companies in the nation. Another brother is a psychiatrist and has been in private practice, a professor at a university, and department chairman of a hospital. My third brother is an engineer, having worked for a major utility company and one of the nation's leading technology firms. And then, there was me. I was supposed to be a lawyer.

My parents were less than excited about my new professional direction. Little fame or money is found in social work. However, as usual, their response was "We just want you to be happy." I was not planning on going to law school, so it appeared my future was wide open.

So I graduated from college with a degree in political science and with no plans for the immediate future. I decided to travel around the United States for a few months. The last two summers I had driven to the East Coast to visit some friends and was anxious to explore the Northwest. Providentially, I ran into Larry, a college friend, in the airport one day and he invited me to visit him in Oregon. He was living with some friends and they were just enjoying the summer. It sounded great to me.

"New" Old Friends

From the first day I drove into Roseburg, Oregon, I fell in love with the Northwest. The trees, streams and mountains all seemed surreal. The colors were beautiful, and it was not even fall. The smell of the trees and the idea of wild-life walking into the yard were stimulating. The first night several deer stood in the front yard. I had seen my share of rattlesnakes, tarantulas and jackrabbits in Arizona; for a city kid from the Southwest, deer and elk in the yard was new and exciting.

I found out quickly that Larry was not the same person I had known. He had recently become a Christian. In fact, the entire household was full of Christians. Larry, Roger, Roger's brother and his wife, Mike and Lori, were calling themselves "born again." Of course, I really did not know what a Christian was, except that they read the Bible, the one with the same stories in every section. Being a "broadminded person," I decided I could handle our differences.

I planned to stay for a few days, a week at the most. I wanted to travel up into Canada. Yet as each day passed I found myself increasingly connected with them. They were kind and truly genuine. Mike and Lori told me to stay as long as I wanted. Amazingly we were laughing, having fun, playing games—all without alcohol, drugs and profanity. It was a new experience for me.

The next three months were some of the most enjoyable times of my life. I found a job in the city and stayed with this "family" for the entire summer. I began to see things in them that I had never seen in anyone else. They genuinely cared about other people. They would stop and help someone change a tire. They made meals for people who were sick. They were honest and refused to take advantage of others. They returned money if given too much change, opened doors for people and helped carry their groceries. Their leisure time was spent praying and singing songs about God. They played games and talked about their future and how they would have an impact on the world. What a culture shock!

We talked late into the nights. They wanted to know what I believed and why I believed it. We talked about faith, God, psychology, philosophy, Judaism, Christianity and Eastern religions. I soon realized that I did not have a real faith foundation. My "moral compass" was severely lacking. I found myself to be a strong proponent of "situational ethics"; my values and morals were dependent upon the situation, the people involved, my moods and whether or not I would benefit personally. I was unsure as to what I believed and how I came to believe it.

I began to ask more questions about Jesus Christ. Their weekly Bible study became a part of my life. I attended their church every Sunday. The worship times were filled with guitar music, clapping hands and expressions of thankfulness to God for His abundance in their lives. I did not understand it all, but I knew something in them was different from any other people I had encountered. They were happy and had an inward peace, something that I lacked.

We started to study the Old Testament and the prophecies proclaimed in the pages of Isaiah, Daniel, Jeremiah and the prophets. From them I learned more about my Jewish heritage and God's plans for the Jewish people than I ever learned from my years in the synagogue. After a couple of months of listening and thinking, I realized this was what I had been looking for years earlier. I had found an answer, but at what cost?

I knew how Jews felt about Christians. Too often Christians, in their apparent zeal for truth, persecuted the Jews. I knew this would jolt the inner workings of my relationship with my family. To speak the name of Jesus Christ was rare, but to be a follower was unheard of in my family. I knew my Jewish friends would "freak out" if they knew I was discussing God and Jesus Christ. The closest we ever came to mentioning God was using profanity.

One night in August 1977, I got out of bed and knelt. As so many others have done, I said, "God, if You are real, I need You. I proclaim that Jesus Christ is Your Son and I want Him to be Lord and Savior in my life." I got back into bed and enjoyed a peaceful, restful night's sleep.

Naturally, my Oregon friends were ecstatic. I stayed there for several more weeks and spent a great deal of time sorting out what this change meant in my life.

The Bottom Falls Out

I returned to Phoenix in late September knowing I needed to talk with my parents. I had spent many hours praying and asking for the right words, knowing the impending discussion could be a disaster. What would this do to my relationship with them? How would my brothers receive it? While concern over their response was strong, at no time did I question my decision. To this day that has never been an issue. Jesus is my Lord and Savior.

The evening of my return was Yom Kippur, the holiest of Jewish holidays. It is the Day of Atonement. Most of the day is spent in the synagogue, speaking prayers and singing. We ask God's forgiveness for sins in our lives and honor our ancestors. It is a solemn and religious occasion. It was after the evening service I asked my parents to sit down and talk.

"I need to have a serious discussion," I said.

My mother looked at me and said cautiously, "You got someone pregnant." I laughed and responded in the negative. She looked more concerned and said, "You are a homosexual." She was obviously losing it. I shook my head and said, "I wish it were that easy." They sat still. The room seemed to be swirling. I took a deep breath, said a silent prayer.

The words formed in my mouth. I stared at my parents, the two most precious people in my life. They were so supportive, so caring. Yet I was about to shatter their lives and knowingly cause them immense pain. Would this destroy our relationship? Would my family continue to be my family or would they "count me as dead"? It was as if time stood still as I prepared to speak the words that would change my life forever.

"I believe Jesus Christ is the Son of God."

Silence—then eruption. Both of my parents were talking, crying, questioning. "We should have sent you to Israel!" "I knew this would happen if you hung around with those friends [meaning non-Jews at college]!" "You need to go talk to the rabbi!" And then my mother's classic words to my father: "Now, Lee," she said. "Don't have a heart attack." Great! I was going to be responsible for Dad's having a heart attack. I had read the story of Lazarus, but I am quite sure I did not have the faith to raise the dead.

The following days were filled with tense discussions, accusations of betrayal and many tears by all. My parents asked me not to tell *anyone* about my new beliefs. They were so ashamed. They could not stand the thought of their friends feeling sorry for them. I agreed not to tell everyone, but I did need to let my brothers know. Though they hesitated at this, they knew they had no choice.

My brothers all responded differently, from indifference to embarrassment. Though it caused a wedge in relationships initially, the following years have brought healing between us.

A Good Move

I moved to the Northwest. The next two years were spent trying to explain my faith to my family, unsuccessfully. Finally I decided to be more of a silent witness and minimize my discussions about God. This was not because God had directed me to do so, but because I wanted to protect myself emotionally. Fear and bondage so gripped my life that I lost my voice to my family. I was afraid to say anything about my faith as it seemed to open old wounds and hurts. Clearly I was intimidated by the emotions generated each time Jesus Christ was mentioned.

My interest in social work took me to a job working with delinquent adolescents at a state correctional facility in Idaho. It was during my time of living in Southeast Idaho that God brought the greatest natural blessing into my life. I met a beautiful young woman who captured my heart. I had never met anyone so completely at peace in life, radiating such beauty both inwardly and outwardly. Yes, I was in love.

Joyce was a single parent with a six-year-old son, Jason. She had become a Christian five years prior and had a deep relationship with God. She was a country girl, having grown up on a farm in Idaho of more than a thousand acres. The majestic Grand Teton Mountains could be seen from her porch. Her childhood memories are filled with horses, snowmobiles, fishing and wide-open spaces.

I played basketball on asphalt; she rode horses in the fields. I walked to the grocery store; she lived fifteen miles from the nearest town. My house was on a block with dozens of other homes; Joyce's nearest neighbor was nearly one mile away. The sun of the summer was as extreme in Phoenix as the snow of winter was in her town of Lamont. Her high school graduating class was smaller than any individual class I took in high school.

She had married at the age of nineteen and had soon had a child. Her relationship with her husband was filled with domestic violence, drug abuse and physical abuse. She would hide enough money for food and diapers each month so that he would not spend it on drugs. After two years of living in fear, she was rescued by her family. They literally came and "kidnapped" her in the middle of the night to avoid the wrath of her husband.

Soon after her divorce she attended a small Christian home meeting. The tenderness and love of the people overwhelmed her. Their singing and praying was a welcome respite from her past few years of emotional distress. However, it was not without its challenges. Joyce tells people, "When I heard people praying out loud I was scared to death. I wanted to run out of the house but I was trapped in the back of the room." Interestingly, she returned the next week. She quickly fell in love with those in the group as well as Jesus Christ. She soon turned her life over to God. Now she had not only a strong natural family but a new church family.

For the next five years she survived as a single mother. She moved back near her family and began going to nursing school. During this time she refused to go out on dates. Even though urged by many of her friends to go and meet people, she believed that this was a time to stay focused on God and allow His healing process to take place in her life.

One exasperated friend said, "Joyce, do you expect that Mr. Right is just going to come and knock on your door?" When Joyce answered confidently in the affirmative, the friend shook her head in disbelief. Amazingly, Joyce and I met when she knocked on my door to ask some questions about the apartments where I lived.

Joyce received her nursing degree in 1978. She applied for a position at a state correctional facility only thirty minutes from her hometown. She was hired immediately. This was the same facility that had hired me only one month earlier.

I watched Joyce while she was dispensing medication to the residents in my cottage. Her gentle, sensitive nature around those hurting, yet difficult, adolescents was amazing. We soon began spending most of our free time with one another. God quickly knit our hearts together.

Her son, Jason, was an active boy who loved his family. He was cautious, at first, about this man who was spending time talking to his mother. Jason had not seen his natural father since the divorce, which left him with a deep father wound. I began to build a relationship with Jason by going sledding, hiking and playing catch.

Finally Free

After the first of the year in 1979, I knew I desired for Joyce (and Jason) to be a permanent part of my life. Though the relationship with my family had settled down, it was still rather tense when the topic of God was brought up. Basically, we just did not talk about my faith. We avoided any discussion of religion, faith or God.

Joyce had little knowledge of Judaism. I had tried to explain the issues surrounding my conversion, but I knew she did not understand. "Mike, I love you and we will work it out" were nice words, but they seemed shallow when I imagined the response from my parents. You see, they hoped that I would "outgrow" this Christian thing. Now that I was talking marriage to a Christian woman, they would know it was real. In February Joyce and I took a trip to visit my parents.

We spent the first evening talking and allowing Joyce to get acquainted. The second day we dug a little deeper. Joyce broke the ice, "I know you don't know me, but I love Mike. We will be happy. I am sure this is a little hard, but I know things will work out." All 4 feet 10 ¾ inches of Mom rose up. She stared at Joyce and me, obviously concerned, hurt and questioning our decision.

The next few hours were less than pleasant. My father and mother tried to convince Joyce and me that we had nothing in common, that the burden of a family would be too great for me at this point of my life. After several days we left determined to be married.

We were married in May. My parents came only because my younger brother, who was my best man, convinced them to come. They cried all the way through the service, and not out of joy. The shame of my Christianity was still fresh in their lives.

I adopted Jason quickly and we became a family. His loving, gentle nature made him a tremendous connecting point for our two families to focus on. Unfortunately, my fear of speaking out about God transferred to Joyce, especially after her experience. We were afraid to say *Christmas, God, church* or anything to do with our faith. If my parents called on a Sunday and wanted to know where we had been that day, we responded that we went out for a drive, leaving out the part about driving to church.

Our wedding bands have the design of a cross on them. We took off our rings when we visited my family. We convinced ourselves it was out of respect, but deep down it was bondage, fear of another blowup. It was horrible; our voices had become silent.

Over the years our children became a bridge to my family—impressing them with their respect for people and kindness. One brother, unsure as to whether or not to have children of his own, commented, "If I knew my children would be like Mike and Joyce's, I would want them." While our relationship with my family got better, we still felt restricted. Conversations were confined to work and kids. We never felt a freedom to talk about our lives, our friends or our dreams.

It took ten years before my parents wished us a "Merry Christmas." I will never forget that letter. "And have a Merry Christmas," it said. You would have thought we had won the lottery. Joyce and I jumped up and down, danced and sang praises to God. It broke something in us. We felt a new freedom in life. No longer did we hide our conversations, take off our rings or let comments sting us. We were free.

We continued to honor and respect my family by not flaunting or pushing our beliefs on them. However, when asked where we were, our response was honest and open. "We were at church" or "We were at a Bible study." Though my family seldom inquired beyond our initial statements, we were confident that our lifestyle of faith and conviction was evident to them.

Now we are able to talk freely about who we are. Discussions of church, mission trips and our faith are part of the family conversations. Though there is still some hesitancy amongst my family, it seems to be slowly changing. And more importantly, we feel free to share our perspectives of life from our godly frame of reference.

One Final Thought . . .

Where once we were in bondage and fear, we found our voices and now openly speak up. No longer are we afraid to be honest regarding church or our dreams in life. This past year, Aaron was in a one-year Bible leadership school. We wrote the entire family, explaining the program and how exciting it was for him. Throughout the year we talked about it with each family member. We continue to grow closer each year. To date no one else has come to the place of recognizing Jesus as his or her Savior. However, we pray and believe each one will experience the excitement, love and truth of God.

Michael Sedler grew up in Phoenix, Arizona. He received his B.A. in political science from the University of California, San Diego, his master of social work from Eastern Washington University, and his doctor of ministry through Christian Life School of Theology. He worked fifteen years in the public school system as teacher, social worker, administrator, and behavior specialist. Following that, Dr. Sedler, an ordained minister, served nine years as an associate pastor. He also worked at a state correctional facility for juveniles and a community mental health agency.

Dr. Sedler grew up in a Jewish home. At the age of thirteen, he had a Bar Mitzvah and, at sixteen, a confirmation. Despite these strong Jewish roots, there was a spiritual longing in his life. The void was filled at the age of twenty-two when God apprehended him. Michael has called Jesus Christ his Lord and Savior ever since.

Through Sedler Ministries, Dr. Sedler travels throughout the United States, ministering in churches and providing consultation services to schools and businesses. He is also an adjunct professor for three universities. He and his wife, Joyce, have developed and presented marriage enrichment seminars for local churches. Together, they have provided countless hours of individual and marriage counseling/guidance.

Dr. Sedler has appeared on radio and television programs throughout the United States and Canada. A frequent seminar speaker, he provides training in the area of communication, motivation, leadership training, and marriage principles.

To contact the author, write to:

Michael Sedler
Sedler Ministries
6505 S. Waneta Road
Spokane, WA 99223
(509) 443-1605
(509) 443-0111 (fax)
email: michael@michaelsedler.com
website: www.michaelsedler.com

Michael Sedler is available for leadership training sessions as well as other speaking engagements such as in-services, church ministry, conferences, or retreats. He is actively involved in training activities throughout the United States and Canada. Dr. Sedler has worked extensively with churches, businesses, and schools. You will find his approach to be both practical and informative.

More on Communication from Dr. Michael D. Sedler

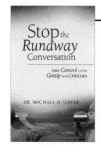

Do Your Conversations Empower or Destroy?
Sticks and stones may break our bones, but words can hurt us, too. Negative speech affects every home, church and workplace. In this book, Dr. Michael Sedler offers insightful strategies for responding biblically to gossip and criticism in your daily life. What do you say when you're caught in an ungodly conversation? How do you avoid speaking harmful words? This powerful book will help you to use words that bring healing and hope and put the brakes on runaway conversations.

Stop the Runaway Conversation by Dr. Michael D. Sedler